ORGANIZE THIS!

Practical Tips, Green Ideas, and Ruminations about your

CRAP

(Clutter that Robs Anyone of Pleasure)

organize your Best Life! Vali

VALI G. HEIST, CPO®

Edited by Sheila Checkoway and Erin Ebersole

Illustrations by Bob Rios
Bob Rios Visual Design
www.brvsdesign.com

ISBN: 1467949175
ISBN 13: 9781467949170

Author's contact information:
Vali G. Heist, M.Ed.
Certified Professional Organizer®
www.thecluttercrew.com
Like me on Facebook
Follow me on Twitter: @ValiOrganize
Leave feedback on Amazon.com

Cover Illustration by Bob Rios
Back Cover Photo by James Cucinotta

To my husband Bob
who puts up with my organizing

To my son Bobby
who has grown up to be a thrower

ACCOLADES FROM VALI'S CLIENTS

"I liked collaborating with Vali on a vision of what my rooms would look like...clutter-free! She helped me to learn how to let go and simplify my spaces."

Single woman working full-time

"With Vali's help I have a completely new home that I am very happy with for the first time in years."

Retired widow

"The professionalism, friendliness, and energy of The Clutter Crew kept us going and the end result was marvelous! I wouldn't have believed we could do it in the time frame you had set out, but we did!"

Retired couple

"Vali is kind of like Mary Poppins! I forget that we're working and the next thing I know, everything has a home."

**Single parent
and full-time Graduate student with one child**

"I'm functioning so smoothly since I completed my work with Vali. She helped me streamline my thoughts, my office, and MY LIFE!"

**Home-based business owner
with husband and four dogs**

"Vali gave me accountability, direction, and future motivation. She improved the use of my garage and my mental state!"

Parent who home-schools four children

"Vali is like having a personal trainer! She keeps me focused and motivated and I am better able to keep my office organized after she leaves."

Single parent working part-time with two children

"It should be a crime to have this much fun!"

Business owner with family of five

CLUTTER THAT

ROBS

ANYONE OF

PLEASURE

crap* \\'krap\\ (2012): *abbr* 1: clutter that robs anyone of pleasure, *n* 2: stuff that does not bring joy, pleasure, usefulness, or life to a home, 2a: owner-specific; one person's crap could be another person's 'treasures', 3: retail or market value is irrelevant, 4: prevents homeowners from enjoying their home or living their best life.

*as defined by Vali G. Heist

CONTENTS

PROLOGUE

A good friend once told me to write my own truth as I know it – and it's a bonus if someone else wants to read it. I was concerned there were so many organizing books already out there but another friend told me to put my own spin on the subject. So, here's my own truth and my own spin on organizing. Use what you can, share this book with a friend, and please send your comments and suggestions for future books. Special thanks to my editors, Sheila Checkoway and Erin Ebersole, for your special gifts and helping me say what I mean. And big thanks to Bob Rios for his unique and fun illustrations. You rock Bob!

Six years ago I read a Redbook magazine article about a woman who started a professional organizing business and I thought "I can do that!" Soon after I quit my full-time job, I started my professional organizing business The Clutter Crew. A few months later I began publishing a monthly column for our local newspaper the Reading Eagle and I've been writing ever since.

In addition to my column, I had an Internet radio program during which I would provide practical tips and ruminations about CRAP. CRAP is an acronym I created that stands for Clutter that Robs Anyone of Pleasure. I used CRAP to describe the mountains of stuff retailers had for sale at Christmas, Halloween, and at any other holiday. When I started my business I realized there's a whole lot more CRAP out there then I previously imagined and it's not just in the stores.

This is not another organizing book to just help you get organized. I will ruminate on why we have so much CRAP, why we don't throw it out, why we can't get to it, and why we don't want to deal with it. I'll try to answer those questions and suggest that if you organize your home even in small ways, it will change your life in big ways. This book is a culmination of my newspaper columns with additional ruminations about CRAP, personal stories, lots of ideas on how to go green with your CRAP, and client success stories to give you hope (names have been changed to protect the organizationally-challenged).

What I knew about myself before I became a professional organizer was that I organized so I could make time to: spend time with friends and family, go forward in my career, read a good book, be spontaneous, sleep late, travel, stay up late, and handle the tough times with grace. This book will explain the meaning behind these words.

What I didn't know about organizing is that it isn't just about having a 'home' for everything: it's about a state of mind and a way of life. It's not about making your home perfect because there's no such thing as perfect (*I don't even like this word*). I also found out that because Americans value CRAP and can't stop buying CRAP, we are putting our planet at risk. Organizing is about recycling, reusing, remixing, and repurposing as a way of life for everyone, not just a few of us. By buying so much CRAP, we also are putting our monetary well-being at risk because we don't have money for important things like education and retirement.

Finally, what I didn't realize when I started my business is how humbled I would be when my clients contact me. They are usually going through some kind of life transition. For some it takes a lot of courage for them to call me; sometimes after years of thinking about it. So to my clients, I thank you for entrusting me to help you with your belongings and thank you for feeding my passion. As Chris Martin, lead singer of the band Cold Play said in an interview on *CBS This Morning* (2011), "My job is a lot of hard work, but I don't have to work hard." Ditto for me.

Thank you for buying my book! Here's to you for aspiring to organize your best life. All the best,

CHAPTER 1

What is CRAP?

Rose loved collecting pigs, but made the mistake
of telling her family and friends.

1.1

Free your space – Free your mind

"A house is just a pile of stuff with a cover on it."

George Carlin, *comedian*

Close your eyes and picture yourself walking into a neat and organized room. How does it make you feel? I ask this question when I give workshops on organizing. I ask the participants to go on a mental journey and talk about clutter, how it affects their physical space, and how it affects their daily lives. Too much physical clutter can suck the life out of our homes and doesn't allow us to breathe or to move forward with our lives. If we fill our lives with stuff, there's no way anything else can come into that space. Peter Walsh, the bestselling author of *It's All Too Much: An Easy Plan for Living a Richer Life with Less Stuff* (2007), says, "If your primary relationship is with your stuff, you are setting yourself up for a life of frustration, because stuff is the worst partner you can have."

We buy stuff because it promises to bring something into our life, but a lot of stuff just ends up taking up space. I call stuff that just takes up space CRAP – Clutter that Robs Anyone of Pleasure. If you aren't using something, it doesn't make you happy, or doesn't make you smile, it's CRAP. However, CRAP is owner-specific – my CRAP isn't necessarily CRAP to someone else. If I give my CRAP to someone else and it becomes useful or makes someone else smile, it's not CRAP: it's just stuff.

> Think about it – each purchase you bring through your front door has strings attached to it and demands attention.

The word clutter comes from the old word 'clotter' meaning to clot or get stuck. When people have too much clutter, homes aren't the relaxing, comfortable places they could be. Too often, stuff is taking over and we are 'stuck' taking care of our stuff. Think about it – each purchase you bring through your front door has strings attached to it and demands attention. It takes time to maintain it, clean it, wash it, dust it, assemble it, repair it, refill it, buy batteries for it, remember you have it, find it, find a home for it, keep track of it, polish it, paint it, freeze it, store it, fold it, file it, find a use for it, use it, iron it, wear it, dry clean it – you get the idea.

The Quaker word 'cumber' is the spiritual weight of having too many material things. The physical clutter that exists in our outer world is a reflection of our inner mental world, which is often an intensely private state of being. Our homes and our private spaces both reflect and affect our emotional well-being. The goal of removing tangible clutter from our homes and our lives is to get rid of what is no longer useful, reopen the flow, stop taking care of or trying to organize CRAP, and make space for living freely and abundantly in the present.

If you are ready to let go of your physical clutter, close your eyes and imagine walking into a neat and organized room. Feel the peace when you are surrounded only by the things you love and are able to find them!

LET'S BREAK IT DOWN:

- Walk through your home and write down how you feel. What emotions are generated when you enter your home and walk into each room? Are these emotions positive or negative?

- Have a dialogue with your clutter (*whisper so the neighbors can't hear*) and find out why it's still there and what you want to do about it.

- Set a timer for 30 minutes or use the clock app on your smartphone. When you are ready to tackle a room go through a small section of the room at a time and unclutter with reckless abandon. When time is up, set the timer for 30 more minutes if you want to keep going.

- Take small steps each week to slowly unearth what's really important to you and contributes to your current life, the life of your home, and the life you want to live.

- Reward yourself along the way by reading a chapter in a book, watching a favorite movie, or taking a long walk with the dog (no retail therapy: that adds to the clutter).

When you free your spaces of CRAP, you can live more in the **present**. Your uncluttered home becomes a place to make room for a better life – not just a pile of stuff with a cover on it. What would you like to have more room for in your life?

SUCCESS IN ACTION

Amelia said she left her house early in the morning and didn't return until it was time to go to bed because she couldn't stand all the clutter. She would spend hours in the library and go out to eat just to avoid her apartment. I asked her what she didn't like about each space including when she walked through the front door. Little by little we worked together to unclutter her spaces so she felt welcome when she came home and could enjoy her home on a daily basis.

1.2

Hoarders: Buried Alive –
Too close to home?

"We tend to confuse the good life with a life of goods."

Simon Schama, *British historian*

"Have you seen the show with those hoarders?" As soon as someone finds out I'm a professional organizer, I get asked this question. I watch the show because it's like a car accident – it's hard to look away. My heart goes out to these people because the pain associated with this disorder is tremendous. Hoarders tend to be reclusive, hiding their amassed possessions from the rest of the world and even their closest friends. I think the hoarding show is so popular because it scares people. I know it's the motivation for some of my clients to call me – they're scared of becoming hoarders.

If someone is truly a hoarder, he or she loses the ability to appraise the worth of things, attaches sentimental value to almost everything, and ends up getting rid of very little. In the book, *Buried in Treasures: Help for Acquiring, Saving and Hoarding* (2007), the authors state that for many people "It took a long time for this problem to build up to its present levels, and it's not going to get better overnight." For hoarders an emotional trigger likely started their downward spiral, and uncluttering requires a psychological component to be successful. The process of uncluttering is not easy or pleasant for a hoarder. The anxiety that results from trying to unclutter can be physically debilitating. On the other hand, the people who call me are overwhelmed by their stuff and are anxious to shed some of their belongings. They want to get rid of CRAP and they realize that their homes and their lives are filled with too much stuff and it's getting in the way of enjoying the good life.

I recommend that anyone who is a hoarder or who might be a hoarder, call a counselor who specializes in hoarding. I also recommend books and websites to help understand hoarding (see Chapter 2.3 and references). Most of us can understand how clutter might get out of control, even if it's not at the hoarder level. We have garages with no room for cars that are filled with equipment we haven't used in years; we have attics filled to the rafters with things we haven't seen in years;

> It's a scary, fine line between a hoarder with a disorder and 'The Great American Consumer' who has too much CRAP.

and we have basements filled with stuff we haven't taken the time to go through in years. It's a scary, fine line between a hoarder with a disorder and 'The Great American Consumer' who has too much CRAP.

Even as the size of the American family has shrunk, the size of a new home has grown because we are buying more and more stuff (see Chapter 8.4). In addition, the number of rented storage spaces has grown exponentially. According to the Self-Storage Association, there were 58,000 self storage facilities worldwide with $20 billion in annual revenues as of June 2011[1]. Many of these facilities have climate-controlled units and electronic key gates – better security than most homes. The tag line for one storage facility company is "Problem Solved!", but is the problem really solved or are the decisions just put on hold?

Traditionally, renters of storage facilities were in transition and only renting for short-term reasons: divorce or relocation; just cleaned out mom and dad's home and didn't know where to go with the stuff; or closed a business and had to store the inventory. But now, renters use these spaces for personal closets, garage and basement overflow, or as an extension of their homes. In some cases, renters go from one storage unit to two then three – the problem isn't solved – it's just put on hold. Many of these units are simply the result of delayed decision-making, and the reality is the renters can accumulate even more clutter, because they've freed up space at home. It's a vicious cycle!

Many of us have the same inclination as a hoarder to hold on to stuff, albeit not as severe. Does this sound familiar: "I know I haven't used it or seen it in years, but…

- I might need it some day."

- I spent a lot for it so I don't want to have to pay to replace it."

- I'm saving it for my kids."

- it's been in the family for years."

- if I get rid of it I'll have to admit it was a bad purchase."

- I'll be able to fix it some day."

- I got it on sale and I can't afford to replace it if I get rid of it."

- I could use it in a craft or art project."

Many professional organizers don't recommend renting storage facilities because it delays decision-making and costs more in the long run. On the other hand, coming to terms with your stuff can be difficult and just plain exhausting. If you are going to tackle a large space or a storage facility, remember: if it took years to get that way, it's not going to take overnight to clean it out. Have patience with yourself and persevere – it can be done!

SUCCESS IN ACTION

When I published a newspaper column referring to the television show on hoarding, I got a number of e-mails about people living with hoarders. Andy sent this response to my column:"I was married to a hoarder for over 30 years and she was the daughter of a hoarder. Our life was mentally, emotionally, and physically exhausting while she made excuses for her problem. Her hoarding problem became my problem. It was a dark secret that our family hid and didn't know how to correct. I finally had to leave. Since I remarried, we keep our home neat and clean. We accept guests unannounced and never fear our home won't be presentable. Life is good, no junk."

I'm not recommending ending a relationship with a hoarder, but what I do recommend is that if you live with a hoarder, find a qualified counselor to talk to and make sure there's at least one room in your home you can call your own.

1.3

Your home and the simplicity of enough

"The voyage of discovery is not in seeking new landscapes, but in having new eyes."

Marcel Proust, *French novelist*

I read a recent news headline that said: "Worst housing market since the 1980's". That same article said that more families are renovating their homes instead of buying new homes. As an organizer I encourage families every day to make their home work for them – instead of against them – whether that means staying in their current home, upgrading their current home, or downsizing to make more room. The size or layout of your home doesn't always matter: it's what you do with the space that counts. My old farm house is small, but it's taught me a lot about maximizing space. I've lived there for almost 30 years.

Sarah Nettleton, an architect, is the author of *The Simple Home, the luxury of enough* (2007). She helps homeowners make the most of their homes by what she calls 'indulging in the simplicity of enough'. Owners of the homes she designs share a common belief that having just enough of the right things is a privilege rather than a compromise. She also says that living simply isn't so much about the stuff you put in your home, but the way your home allows you to enjoy the simple pleasures of life and celebrate the luxury of your own version of 'enough'.

> The size or layout of your home doesn't always matter: it's what you do with the space that counts.

Many of us have the opposite of enough which is too much. And most of us may not have the best of everything, but is that necessarily the goal in life? Nettleton talks about the prosperity of needing less: that simple thrift is about more than saving money. The word 'thrift' is historically tied to the word 'thrive', which in the 14th century thrift meant the condition of thriving and prosperity. This is a far cry from the negative words we associate with thrift such as doing without or budget-driven – but thrifty can be a good thing!

Coincidentally, Sarah Susanka is another architect who points to organizing your home and your life as one of the essential ways to lessen stress in good times and bad. She is the author of the book, *the not so big life: making room for what really matters* (2007). She writes about being conscious of whatever you are doing in your home and being conscious of why you are doing it. Instead of overstuffed houses and overstuffed lives, she encourages us to make room for what we long to have time for. She suggests that we slow down, do with less, and live in the present. Building a bigger home to fit more CRAP is not my idea of making room for what really matters.

If you are postponing buying a new home for any reason, maybe a fresh perspective from a professional organizer or a realtor could help. Perhaps some reorganizing, redecorating, or renovating your existing home is what is needed to help you stay there, enjoy it more, and make it work for you.

LET'S BREAK IT DOWN:

- Goals. Write down your family's goals for your home. Your list will provide the basis for the future decisions you make to change your home. For example, spend money to improve your home; limit spending, but improve your home;

get ready for in-laws to visit; have family in for a long summer visit; or invite the extended family for a Thanksgiving meal.

- Home Walk-Through. Use a separate sheet of paper for each room and write everything down. Begin by walking in the front door. How do you feel? How would you like to feel? Try to see your home through the eyes of a stranger. Invite someone to go through with you.

- List the Positives. List what you like about each room, e.g. the layout, the furniture, the sunlight that comes through the windows in the morning, the color of the walls, etc.

- List the Negatives. List what you don't like, e.g. the layout, too much furniture, too much clutter, not enough bookcases, the color of the walls, the décor, etc.

- Stuff/Clutter. Take a good look at all the stuff in each room. Is there too much? Do you just need bookcases or containers to hold it? Does all this clutter fit in with the goals for the future of this space or your family? How long has it been since you've identified whether you love or need each thing in the room?

- Repairs and Changes. List all repairs or changes, e.g. repair door handle, caulk windows, change curtains, add a desk for office space, change paint color, unload extra furniture, etc.

- Prioritize Your Lists. According to your budget and a timeline, decide which changes should be made first and go from there.

You'll be surprised how a few key changes can make a huge difference in your attitude when you walk into your home or into each room of your home. On the other hand if you are unhappy with your home because you are unhappy with your life, that's a whole different matter – discern the difference. Instead of changing your landscape by moving, maybe looking at your home with new eyes will give you a new perspective. After shedding the extra clutter and reworking your spaces, your home will feel brand new! If you decide to move at a later date, you'll be taking the things with you that bring meaning, not dread, to your life.

SUCCESS IN ACTION

Barb and her husband were going to build a larger home, but plans had to be postponed indefinitely because of job concerns. In order to stay in their current home and accommodate three children, I worked with her to identify what wasn't working and brainstormed about how to change each room. The process involved a lot of uncluttering and reorganizing of spaces so they could live comfortably in their present home until they were ready to revisit building a larger home.

1.4
Keeping clutter at bay

*"Have nothing in your house that you do not know to be useful
or believe to be beautiful."*

William Morris, *English textile designer*

I taught a class on organization several times at the local
community college and one topic I covered was the Physics of
Clutter. Rule #1 is that it doesn't take a lot of effort on our part
for clutter to come in to our homes. First, the majority of our
mail is unsolicited. Second, much of the stuff we accumulate is
a result of normal (or American) consumption. It's become
second nature to keep bringing stuff in the door without much
thought to how it got there. The normal consumer habits are
causing us, our homes, and our planet lots of stress by
accumulating more and more stuff. Before I teach students
how to organize their stuff, we start by understanding where
all the clutter is coming from.

Much of our accumulated clutter is
from 'retail therapy'. The definition
of retail therapy is shopping with
the primary purpose of improving
the buyer's mood or disposition.
Typically, it is a short-lived habit and
the term was first used in the Chicago
Tribune on Christmas Eve in 1986:
"We've become a nation measuring
out our lives in shopping bags and
nursing our psychic ills through retail therapy." But with the
U.S. consumer debt growing larger each year to a total of $2.43

> The normal
> consumer habits
> are causing
> us, our homes,
> and our planet
> lots of stress by
> accumulating
> more and more
> stuff.

trillion as of May 2011[2], retail therapy is no longer a short-lived habit – it's a primary source of entertainment.

Our homes are finite entities even though we try to fill them beyond capacity – there's only so much room. Remember, everything we bring through our doors has to be dealt with in some way. And if we never take anything out of our home, it will be hard to locate what we really want amidst all the stuff. You shouldn't have to push anything out of the way to get to what you really want. The key to keeping clutter at bay is learning to limit what we bring through the door and making sure stuff is going out.

LET'S BREAK IT DOWN:

Mail – the biggest perpetrator of clutter:

- Have a 'mail sorting station' located wherever you bring in the mail. Keep a large trash can, recycle bin, and shredder by that station.

- Throw out junk mail immediately. Rip up all credit card offers. Shred anything with current account numbers and social security numbers.

- Opt-out of junk mail. See Chapter 4.1 for suggestions.

Errands – run errands to remove items from your home:

- Errands can include dry cleaning, items to exchange at stores, items to return to people, banking, post office, repairs, etc.

- Place items in a basket or an area by the door you exit to take out when you leave. Better yet, put them in the car.

- Accumulate your errands and get them done in one day to save time. Or run errands on your way home from work to save gas.

Free/Cheap/Bargain/On Sale – sales are a dime a dozen:

- Learn to resist! Just because an item is free, inexpensive, or on sale doesn't mean you need it.

- Be selective if you shop at yard sales or thrift stores. Ask yourself if this 'must have' item is on the list of things you really need.

- Buy items at yard sales to replace something you already have (upgrade), or buy items you can sell on eBay to make money.

Gift Giving – think experiences, not stuff:

- Make memories instead of buying stuff – dinner, a movie, a museum visit, or a Broadway show. See Chapter 6.2 for more suggestions.

- Give savings bonds (purchase online at www.treasury-direct.gov) or contribute to 529 college savings plans in the name of the student.

- Regifting is okay. Once it's yours, you may do with it what you wish.

New in/Old out – when stuff comes in, take stuff out:

- Always recycle, sell, or donate the old model/item when you buy something new, especially electronics.

- Obtain a receipt for your taxes if you donate items to a nonprofit organization.

Organize This!

- Don't put the old item in the attic, garage, basement, or that 'extra' room (yes, we all have one).

Clothing – most people wear 20% of what's in their closets:

- Try clothing on before you buy. Return items if they don't fit or work with your wardrobe.

- Let go of something you'll no longer choose to wear when you bring in new clothing. Don't buy any new hangers. Recycle dry cleaning hangers.

- Choose classic items and use accessories to update your wardrobe.

Make Lists – saves money and time:

- Keep a list for groceries, birthdays, clothing, household items, etc. I keep a list in my iPhone.

- Take stock of what you have before you make a list of the items you need when preparing for parties and holiday gatherings.

- Make a wish list of items you need and want. Keep on your Smartphone.

Beware of HSN, QVC, catalogs, and 24/7 Internet shopping:

- Beware of these 'home invaders': they want to sell you something you don't need, don't have money for, or don't have room for.

- Look out for the overused word 'collectible'. This word implies that someday the item will be worth more than you paid for it or you need to buy every piece to have the full collection.

- Don't leave QVC or HSN on the television for background noise. It's too much of a temptation to buy CRAP. Try the weather channel or music channels.

Finally, have a 'home' for everything. Without a home, things just lie around and become CRAP. Take a few moments each day to put things away – you will save hours down the road. If the things in your home are no longer beautiful or useful, do a little maintenance each week to remove these things and keep the clutter at bay.

SUCCESS IN ACTION

Greg was aware that he was buying too much stuff and his home was becoming cluttered because he didn't know where to put everything. We talked about where all the clutter was coming from (delayed decisions and overbuying) and we worked together in his home to let go of the things he wasn't using and didn't need. I taught him to take a list when he shops and now he buys much differently because he makes sure he has a use for an item before he takes it home. Knowing that each purchase has strings attached (find a home or a use for something) made a big impression on him.

1.5

Top ten myths for not unloading CRAP

"Whoever has the most stuff leaves a mess for the relatives."

Vali G. Heist

As a professional organizer, I know that the first step to getting organized is taking away the excess CRAP. Organizing and making room for stuff that you haven't used, you don't want, or stuff that isn't contributing to the life of your home can be like rearranging the deck chairs on the Titanic. There are so many excuses (a.k.a. myths) for why we believe we can't let go of items we aren't using or don't need. Not that these excuses aren't valid, but when you are dealing with an overwhelming amount of belongings, dispelling those myths is critical and will lead to successful purging of CRAP.

Donna Smallin, author of *Organizing Plain & Simple* (2002), says that purging excess CRAP involves a thought process. She says that "organizing requires you to think about what's most important to you – what you really love and want – and to make decisions based on that knowledge." Understanding who you are, where you are in your life, and why you want to organize can motivate you to begin the process and work toward a defined goal. Without that thought process, purging can be difficult and unstructured.

> Sometimes it takes a total paradigm shift to see our belongings for what they really are: CRAP.

I believe that most excuses for not getting rid of CRAP fall under the emotional categories of guilt, insecurity, and fear. Some feel guilty about letting go of something someone gave to them or they feel insecure that the decisions to get rid of clutter will come back to haunt them. Many are afraid they will need something as soon as they get rid of it (*that's an urban legend by the way*). Sometimes it takes a total paradigm shift to see our belongings for what they really are: CRAP. As I work with clients to achieve their goals, we find out why they are holding on to stuff they don't use or don't even want. As a result, the excess stuff begins to fall away.

If you need help unloading your clutter, here's how to dispel those myths one by one. I ordered them in the familiar top ten style a la David Letterman.

LET'S BREAK IT DOWN:

Number 10 – "I might need it someday."

If you haven't used something in two years, it is clutter. This is just a guideline, but if clutter is in the way of achieving your goals – donate it, sell it, give it away, or recycle it. See Chapter 6 for how to go green with your CRAP.

Number 9 – "It cost a lot of money!"

That doesn't mean you can't let it go. Keeping the item around is a constant reminder of how much you paid for it and that you aren't using it. Give it to someone who needs it or sell it and get some of your money back.

Number 8 – "A friend gave it to me."

A gift means it belongs to you and you can do anything you want with it. That means giving it to someone else who will use it, regifting it, or donating it.

Number 7 – "My aunt gave it to me and I want to display it when she comes to visit."

How often does she visit and do you think she'll remember she gave it to you? You are placing a burden on yourself to keep track of that item for only that purpose.

Number 6 – "It's been in my family for years."

Family heirlooms are meant to be used and honored. That's not happening if the stuff sits in your basement, attic, or storage facility. If you love it and it's important to you, use it in your home. If you don't love it or can't use it, pass it on to someone who will use it.

Number 5 – "I'm going to pass it down to my kids."

Don't assume anyone wants your stuff (a.k.a. antiques) unless you ask. If the answer is no: no means no. If someone does want it and you no longer need it, give it as a gift for a birthday or a holiday and watch the recipient delight in your gift now.

Number 4 – "My kids might need it someday and I have the room to store it."

Many parents hold on to stuff for their children to use when they move out on their own, especially household items. That extra toaster, crock pot, sofa, or set of dishes has a 'shelf' life; so if your kids don't need it for two years, donate it. Some items break down over time: you may eventually have to throw it out.

Number 3 – "I'm saving it for my grandchildren."

Do you even have grandchildren? How do you know they will want it? Will you be able to find the item if and when that time comes? The greatest gift for grandchildren is your time…or savings bonds.

Number 2 – "My children will get rid of all this stuff when I'm gone."

Ask people who have cleaned out their parent's home and they will tell you it was emotionally complicated and physically exhausting. Some families are forced to rent a dumpster and throw things into the landfill just because it's too overwhelming to go through it piece by piece.

And the **Number 1** reason why people don't get rid of CRAP – "But it's so cute!"

You're killing me! If it's so cute, then why aren't you using it? Donate it to a charity, sell it on consignment or on eBay, give it away to someone who needs it or wants it, or recycle it responsibly.

If your clutter is starting to give you a headache, don't make excuses. Take action. When you stop justifying the existence of your clutter, it's easier to let go of the emotion attached to the item and the item itself. Don't leave a mess for your relatives – if you begin uncluttering while you are able, your children will thank you for it.

SUCCESS IN ACTION

Erin said she wanted to save her old childhood books for her grandchildren. Her children were only five and six years old, and her old books were already worn and tattered. After discussing where to keep the books so that in 20-something years she would be able to locate them, we decided to donate them to children who currently had no books. She was relieved that she wouldn't have to keep track of the books. Donating them made so much more sense.

CHAPTER 2

The Basics of CRAP

Coaching four sports gave Bob hours of joy and
hundreds of t-shirts he'll never wear again.

2.1

Where did all this CRAP come from?

*"Chinese factory worker can't believe
all the shit he makes for Americans."*

headline from the book *The Onion*

Did you ever wonder how you got all the stuff that is cluttering your home? Many of my clients do. When clients call me to assist them with uncluttering their homes, it really is a mystery to them and many are embarrassed. There are many answers to this question, but first and foremost, life is busy. Whether you are a single parent or have a partner, work in or out of the home, have 1.5 kids or a dog and a cat thrown in – you've got a home full of activity – and not a lot of time for organizing.

> We can blame China for manufacturing most of the stuff we buy, but Americans ask for it as fast as the Chinese can make it.

On the other hand, the mother of all culprits for why we accumulate crap is advertising. Department store sales, home shopping networks, and Internet shopping keep us buying the next best thing. We can blame China for manufacturing most of the stuff we buy, but Americans ask for it as fast as the Chinese can make it. When I was an undergraduate marketing major, I learned to spot all the tricks of the advertising trade: e.g. playing on our insecurities to get us to purchase a product. If a commercial makes a bold claim about 'changing your life' or some such nonsense, I voice my opinion at home. My young son would hear the same commercial days later and respond to the announcer by saying, "Yeah, right!"

In a book published by The New Democracy Forum called *Do Americans Shop Too Much?* (2000), one of the contributing authors Betsy Taylor notes that "Americans feel enormous pressure to acquire things as the only avenue for gaining love, respect, and a sense of belonging." This pressure results in a vicious cycle of working longer hours to acquire more stuff – but having less time to enjoy those material goods. Finally, many people develop an emotional attachment to their clutter, and don't let it go because stuff keeps memories (good and bad) and self-respect alive (*that's scary*). And even though we may not use or need a lot of our stuff, we don't want to get rid of it because it's still 'good' – and throwing it away would be wasteful.

When is it time to get rid of the clutter (a.k.a. CRAP)?

- You walk into your home, heave a big sigh and consider getting on a plane and never coming back – it's time.

- You're overwhelmed by the sheer volume of your stuff. You can't breathe. It's just all too much – it's time.

- If clutter is looming large (pun intended) and it's causing you to misplace things, miss appointments, and pay bills late – it's time.

- You buy items twice because you can't find the first one you bought (no, you are not the only one) – it's time.

- Your clutter feels like a personal failure as opposed to something that needs to be taken care of – it's time.

How do you get rid of the clutter once you decide it must go?

- Commit to the task: Set aside blocks of time to complete the task. Put it in your day planner, smartphone, or task list.

- Start small: Think plastic food container drawer in the kitchen or bookshelf in the family room – don't tackle the whole house.

- Sort first: Put things in common groups; like with like. That's the only way to tell how much of each thing you have.

- Divide into categories: keep, donate, give away, and throw away (see Chapter 6.1).

- Recruit a friend to assist you if the task is too large for one person.

If you want to unclutter and it gives you heart palpitations as opposed to a good feeling, call a professional organizer. You'll need some assistance to get the job done because making decisions about what to let go can be difficult. Finding out why you buy so much stuff may also need to become a part of the process. You'll also get resources for where to take items to recycle and donate. There is hope!

SUCCESS IN ACTION

Michael felt disorganized, had a lot of stuff in his home, and wasn't sure why he was keeping all his stuff. We talked about his circumstances growing up, how long he was in his current home, where a lot of his items came from, and what it might be like if he let go of his unneeded items. We got to the root of his disorganization and the clutter started to fall away. After a few sessions together, Michael was able to unclutter on his own. Everyone has different issues with clutter. The goal is to unearth those issues and move past them.

2.2

Organizing saves money
in any economy

"You rarely have time for everything you want in this life,
so you need to make choices.
And hopefully your choices can come from a deep
sense of who you are."

Fred Rogers, a.k.a. Mr. Rogers, *educator and television host*

I have vivid childhood memories of my mother taking me to the Goodwill Retail Store to shop – and I wasn't happy about it. I wanted to shop at the mall like my friends, but we didn't have a lot of money so our options were limited. As an adult, I had to make choices on how to spend my limited budget so thrift stores became a welcome way of life. When my son was young I took him to the Goodwill. He enjoyed going to these stores because he could get more for his money when shopping for toys. As a teenager, he would call to tell me what great bargains he found at the local thrift store while shopping with friends. He learned the value of a dollar and how far he could stretch it.

Lately the news headlines have reflected the state of the economy. I've seen headlines such as: "Fewer workers eat lunch out" and "Consumers changing spending habits". When I can't control the price of gas or food, I try to take control of the little things that save money and make a difference on a daily basis. In the book *Frugillionaire: 500 Fabulous Ways to Live Richly and Save a Fortune* (2009), author Francine Jay says that saving a few dollars here and there can add up to big bucks by mastering the art of frugality – living richly while saving a fortune. All it takes is a few good habits and a new perspective.

> Buying used (or previously enjoyed) is not just about saving money – it's a smart way to shop.

Not only do I make shopping at thrift stores a habit, I volunteer with Goodwill Industries to support the programs for people with disabilities and other challenges to live independent lives. Goodwill also supports youth employment and mentoring programs. Look for a nonprofit thrift store in your community to support by buying items, donating unneeded stuff, and volunteering your time. Buying used (or previously enjoyed) is not just about saving money – it's a smart way to shop. In any economy, organizing can save money by allowing time to plan ahead and change some habits.

LET'S BREAK IT DOWN:

Make lunches from dinner:

- Make a few extra servings at dinner and freeze the leftovers in pint containers (pint butter containers work well).

- Use one protein, one vegetable, and one starch and add a pat of butter for moisture when reheating (*I saved big bucks doing this!*).

- Store pre-made lunches in a separate place in the freezer for easy retrieval in the morning.

- Freeze restaurant leftovers for lunches.

Plan meals ahead of time:

- Save time and gas by going to the grocery store only once a week.

- Plan the week's menu by using what's on hand and only buying perishables.

- See websites for planning meals at www.mealsmatter.org and www.e-mealz.com.

- Download meal planning apps for a smartphone: *Meal Planning* or *MealBuilder Pro*.

- Buy in bulk if you have room to store it, you won't forget you have it, and it won't go to waste.

- Save eating out for special occasions to save money.

Make a list before you shop:

- Take stock of supplies before you shop. Make a detailed list or print lists from websites and check off what you need.

- Keep 'needs' and 'wants' separate. Advertisers can create needs you didn't know you had.

- Buy only to replace something that is used up, worn out, or broken beyond repair.

- Keep birthdates, clothing sizes, and gift ideas in your wallet or on a smartphone to avoid buying unwanted gifts (a.k.a. CRAP).

Coupons and discounts:

- Clip coupons only for the items you use often. Organize them by the aisles in the grocery store to save time.

- Look for coupons online: www.shopathome.com, www.coupons.com, www.couponcabin.com, and www.couponmom.com.

- Keep discount cards, coupons, and gift cards in one envelope in your handbag or in the car so you remember to use them.

- Download the app *Key Ring Reward Cards* to scan and save cards on your smartphone. Reward/loyalty cards that offer an immediate discount are worth using – others are just a nuisance.

Consolidate errands to save gas:

- Return items to the store that don't work or don't fit ASAP. Place them by your home's exit door to remember to follow through.

- Run errands on the way home from work and in the order of their location to save gas. Write it down to remember (*I do!*).

Get the kids involved:

- Talk to your children about the daily decisions you make to save money.

- Ask them for their opinion when you compare prices or make small money decisions.

- Point out and explain unit pricing on store shelves when you grocery shop.

Spending and saving money is all about making choices. For one week challenge yourself and your family to limit spending money unless you absolutely must – talk about every purchase.

See how much money you have left at the end of the week, and do something memorable with the money to celebrate. Could a little organizing save you big bucks?

SUCCESS IN ACTION
Pat had three young children and decided to leave her job so she could stay home and care for them full-time. As a result money was tight and coupon clipping became a necessary obsession. We worked together to organize her coupons so it was easy to shop at her favorite grocery store. We bookmarked all the coupon websites and she passed on her wisdom to her extended family on how to save their hard-earned money. She now saves an average of $50 per week for her family.

2.3

Plenty of help for the organizationally-challenged

"I believe pain is an essential motivating tool in the quest to better one's life…no one moves who's not in enough pain."

Kenny Loggins, *singer and songwriter*

When I started my business in 2005 there were 2,500 professional organizers ready and able to help people conquer their clutter. I remember attending the National Association for Professional Organizers conference in Boston, Massachusetts and thinking, "I have found my people". Six years later, there are over 4,200 organizers in 12 countries, and the number of cable television shows about organization is ever increasing. When I'm at a gathering and people find out I'm a professional organizer, they usually tell me they know someone who could use my help: an in-law, a parent, or a neighbor. Some are even brave enough to admit they could use help to unclutter their own homes.

Some of my clients fall into special categories that hinder their efforts at becoming organized. These can include ADD (Attention Deficit Disorder), chronic disorganization, physically disabled, hoarders, elderly, students, and children. Kolberg and Nadeau are authors of the book *ADD-Friendly Ways to Organize Your Life* (2002). It includes strategies that really

Regardless of your status as a keeper of stuff (or CRAP) there is a plethora of information available to assist you.

work written by a professional organizer and a renowned ADD clinician. The authors know that organizing doesn't make sense for everyone and many find it difficult to conquer clutter and organize. The first chapter of their book is called 'A Different Organizing Approach', which is exactly how some people need to approach organizing – differently.

Not every professional organizer is an expert at helping people who fall into all these categories. It is important to locate one who has dealt with clients who are like you. Go to the National Association of Professional Organizers (www.napo.net) or Certified Professional Organizers® (www.certifiedprofessionalorganizers.org) websites, enter your zip code, and locate an organizer in your location with the expertise you desire. Also, if you decide to elicit the help of a therapist, find someone who specializes in your specific difficulty. These professionals will listen to your concerns, assess your situation, and provide the help you need.

Regardless of your status as a keeper of stuff (or CRAP) there is a plethora of information available to assist you. I have created a list of resources in the back of this book with names of books, websites, and smartphone apps to assist you with organizing your belongings or your life. These resources are continually recommended by professional organizers because they provide helpful information to the organizationally-challenged. Find the ones that speak to you (I hope this book does!) and move your life forward. Here is my list of the most helpful websites on organizing.

LET'S BREAK IT DOWN:

- Online Organizing at www.onlineorganizing.com. This site is chock full of information including finding an organizer, a store of organizing products, free newsletters, links, advice, and professional organizer blogs (like mine!).

- International OCD Foundation at <u>www.ocfoundation.org/hoarding</u>. If you or someone you know is a hoarder, go to this website for definitions, community resources, and hope for hoarders and those living with hoarders.

- The Clutter Crew at <u>www.thecluttercrew.com</u>. This is my business website which includes links to my current newspaper columns and tip sheets you can download for free. Complete the contact form if you'd like to sign up for my monthly eNewsletter.

- The Clutter Diet at <u>www.theclutterdiet.com</u>. Receive online consulting from pros, a weekly 'menu' plan of organizing projects, multimedia tutorials, articles, and other great tools…all for an affordable cost.

- Clutterers Anonymous (CLA) at <u>www.clutterersanonymous.net</u>. This website includes a fellowship of people who share their experience, strength, and hope with each other to solve their common problem with clutter and help each other to recover. The only requirement for membership is a desire to stop cluttering. There are no dues or fees for membership.

- Clutterless Recovery Groups, Inc. at <u>www.clutterless.org</u>. The author of this site started developing uncluttering programs to help chronically disorganized clutterers in 1998. Clutterless Recovery Groups are not professional organizers or psychological professionals, but their philosophy can complement the work of professionals.

- Fly Lady at <u>www.FlyLady.net</u>. Marla Cilley is The Fly Lady and FLY stands for Finally Loving Yourself. She is the author of the successful system of conquering CHAOS (Can't Have

Anyone Over Syndrome) by working in zones and taking baby steps to conquer clutter in the home.

- Messies Anonymous at www.messies.com. Sandra Felton, The Organizer Lady®, gifted speaker and accomplished author, is the Messies Anonymous founder. Her site provides support for Messies who struggle to control clutter at home and work.

- National Study Group on Chronic Disorganization at www.nsgcd.org. Their mission is to benefit people affected by chronic disorganization. The NSGCD explores, develops and communicates information, organizing techniques and solutions to professional organizers, related professionals and the public.

If your life and your home are unorganized to the point of causing you emotional and physical pain, there is help out there. Organizing tools – whether it's a professional organizer, book, website or app – are available to help you organize your home and your life to the level that you want to and deserve to be organized. You can do this!

SUCCESS IN ACTION

Camryn was having trouble letting go of a backlog of childhood belongings. In addition, she was buying many new items online for her children and her home was becoming overwhelmed with clutter. Through a combination of sessions with a professional counselor and uncluttering with me in her home, she was able to begin clearing the items she no longer needed and would never use again. Camryn realized she was at the beginning of her journey to unclutter, but she was committed to additional visits with a counselor and realized that it was a process, not a destination.

2.4

A clean desk sparks a creative mind

"Early in my career I felt that organization would destroy my creativity; whereas now, I feel the opposite. Discipline is the concrete that allows you to be creative."

Verna Gibson, *retail tycoon*

You know the old saying: "A clean desk is the sign of a sick mind". Well, the lady doth protest! In my former career as a higher education administrator, my colleagues made fun of my clean desk: the truth is I still can't focus on a project or be creative without a clean palette. I found this especially true as I wrote this book! Many of my clients want a quiet place to be creative or a work area that is uncluttered so they can begin to work at a moment's notice. When inspiration strikes, you shouldn't have to search for a space or unearth a flat surface in order to write, scrapbook, sew, read a book, paint, or just meditate. Your time is precious and you deserve better.

> Many talented people are able to create anything and everything – except order.

Some of my creative clients (a.k.a. right brain thinkers), such as teachers and artists, have trouble keeping their desks or work areas clear because they have so much stuff. On one hand, they feel that organizing their work area will stifle their creativity. On the other hand, they are desperate to bring some order to their spaces because it takes so long to get going. In the book, *Organizing for the Creative Person* (1993) by Lehmkuhl and Lamping, the authors explain that many talented people are able to create anything and everything – except order.

"Despite their many exceptional abilities, they have a hard time attending to details, keeping things where they belong, finding what they need, getting to places on time, following through on projects, and so on."

To complicate matters, creative minds tend to keep a lot of stuff because they see the possibilities in everything: a scrap of paper, an article in a journal, a picture in a magazine, a bottle cap, or a piece of ribbon. As a result, inventory is huge and keeping it organized is a real challenge. By the time they clear the clutter and find what they want to work on, they are worn out.

If your messy desk is keeping you from being creative or you are exhausted from just getting started, you need assistance.

LET'S BREAK IT DOWN:
Location, location, location:

- Think 'prime real estate': these are the areas closest to your work space. Keep things you use daily or weekly close to or on your work space. If items are rarely used, store them elsewhere.

- Try not to combine your work/office area with a bedroom or a kitchen. Kitchens are generally the hub of the home and bedrooms are for sleeping.

- Use a room screen to separate different zones for different uses. Screens are great when you have a small home or you must multipurpose a room.

- Post the rules of the area so everyone who uses it keeps it organized. If the craft room is used by children, posted rules are a must.

Categorize first:

- Group 'like' items together to see how much you have of each 'thing'.

- If needed items are located elsewhere in your home, bring it all into one place.

- Throw away or donate items that haven't been used in the last two years – clear the CRAP.

- Categorize by color if you work by color. Categorize by type of medium if you work with different mediums.

- Pare down your items if you have too many so they are manageable, or move some to another location.

Containerize next:

- Choose the type of container by the way you use the items; e.g. if you use items often, such as paper clips, don't use a lid for the container.

- Use clear containers as opposed to opaque if you need to see what's in the container.

- Use items you already own as containers especially if the item invokes a happy feeling (e.g. a vase from a friend, tea cup from a grandparent, coffee cup from a special vacation).

- Use containers to make clean up easier.

- Think 'up'. Use the walls to hang items and unclutter surfaces.

Maintain continually:

- Resist dumping. When you bring new things into your work area, put them away.

- Clean up after you are done for the day so that when you approach the space next time, you are ready to get down to business.

- Don't be afraid to change the system if it starts to break down or becomes cumbersome.

- Be stingy about the things you commit to keeping. Everything comes with strings attached and you'll have to keep track of it.

Organization is a good thing: it means freedom – not conformity. Organizing doesn't have to stifle your creativity. With a little discipline your spaces will be ready to go when you are. If you get to work faster and work more efficiently, you'll become more creative in the process. Get those creative juices flowing!

SUCCESS IN ACTION

I worked with Margaret in her artist's workshop where she created items for her business. She had a lot of trouble locating her tools every time she sat down to work. We looked at each item in her workshop, and I asked her how and if she used it. Little by little we moved items where they were used, rather than where they were dropped or deposited in haste. We categorized, containerized, and found a permanent home for everything. Margaret called me weeks later to tell me she was thriving in her new space because her tools were easy to locate when she was ready to work and easy to put away for the next work session.

2.5

Understand your brain to stay organized

*"Any fool can make things bigger, more complex,
and more violent. It takes a touch of genius and a lot of
courage to move in the opposite direction."*

Albert Einstein, *German physicist*

Your brain works best when you focus on one thing at a time. Consider this imagined scenario involving NCIS (my favorite television show): Tony Dinozzo's director Leon Vance called him into his office and said, "There's a murderer on the loose. I want you to shoot first and ask questions later!" Tony pulls out his gun, shoots Leon full of holes, and then asks, "What does he look like?" The moral of the story: if Tony had slowed down and focused on what Leon was saying, he wouldn't have shot him. Slowing down to focus isn't in our nature and our brains know that.

> Slowing down to focus isn't in our nature and our brains know that.

Chris Crouch, author of *Being Productive: Learning how to get more done with less effort* (2009), explains that when you overload your brain by rushing, taking on too many tasks, or operating under too much stress, your emotional brain takes over and starts calling the shots. To stay organized, good habits and cues are essential to being productive so your thinking brain can get things done. Slowing down also heightens your sense of awareness. Without a combination of good habits, cues and slowing down, the thinking functions of your brain shut down, you default to your old habits, and life again becomes a complex world that feels out of control.

You know the old saying, "The squeaky wheel gets the grease?" Well, that's our brain responding to the noise around us instead of us taking control of our actions. I work with clients every day to change habits and start new ones in order to get and stay organized. Whether we set up a new filing system, organize the garage, or reorganize the kitchen – starting a new habit takes at least 30 days to take hold. To **stay** organized – maintenance is the key.

Here are the top ten tips I give to my clients after we've set up a system to help them keep their spaces organized. Again, I have listed them a la David Letterman:

LET'S BREAK IT DOWN:

Number 10 – Trust your judgment

Trust your instincts and don't second guess yourself. Your lifestyle and preferences will tell you how to move forward. Don't let others decide for you.

Number 9 – Commitment

Pledge to the organizing process. Trust the work you've done. Give the process time to fully work in your life.

Number 8 – Maintenance

Set regular time on your calendar (daily, weekly, monthly – whatever works for you) for maintenance. Put things back, hang up clothing, throw out the trash, and wipe down surfaces.

Number 7 – New habits

Continue to practice good habits and let go of the old ones. Remind yourself of how good you feel when you are organized.

Number 6 – Be thankful

Encourage family members as often as necessary when they work to keep spaces organized. Acknowledge their contributions when they keep areas neat.

Number 5 – No digging

You shouldn't have to unearth or search for what you really need. Keep most-used items front and center. If it doesn't have a home, give it one.

Number 4 – Constantly purge

If you didn't already designate one, keep a bag/box/wash basket handy to deposit items you and your family no longer need or want (I keep mine in the bedroom). Donate regularly: No more CRAP.

Number 3 – One bite at a time

If you feel overwhelmed, break a larger project into smaller, manageable tasks. Stay focused until you are ready to move on to the next task.

Number 2 – Invite company

Welcome people into your home regularly. You'll be motivated to keep your home organized.

And the **Number 1** tip to keeping your spaces organized – If it takes less than 60 seconds, just do it!

When you let all the little things go, they become big things. If you don't take time to do it now, you'll have to find time later.

Finally, Chris Crouch says that "Understanding how your brain works enables you to exercise some control over it instead of it controlling you." Remember you are not alone when you have to challenge (or trick!) your brain to get things done. You know what will work for you in order to get things done – have the courage to do it.

SUCCESS IN ACTION

After I organized with Harper in her home, she was able to take her newly learned skills with her while visiting her mother who lived in another state. She helped her mom downsize and move to an assisted-living facility. She encouraged her mother to trust her judgment and worked with her to take one step at a time to downsize a lifetime of belongings. Patience and understanding were easier to invoke because Harper now had the appropriate skills to work with her mom.

CHAPTER 3

Home CRAP-free Home

Aunt Grace's collection of antique dolls was impressive,
but gave everybody else the creeps.

3.1

Tips for a carefree closet

*"The garment hanging in your wardrobe
is the garment of him who is naked;
the shoes that you do not wear
are the shoes of the one who is barefoot."*

St. Basil the Great, *Christian theologian*

For 24 years I worked in a professional office environment. I purged my closets twice a year of unneeded clothing – end of the winter and end of the summer. Frequently I invited my close friend who worked at the same company to sit on my bed and give me her honest opinion while I tried on each piece. Her honesty was indispensable so I could make real changes in my wardrobe and purge the stuff that was too old, didn't look great, or was just out of style. She gave me permission to let go of my CRAP.

> All women deserve carefree closets because they make us feel good about our bodies no matter the size or shape.

Regardless of size or age, women (and most men!) want their clothing to be in fashion and reflect their individual style. However, as we age or fluctuate in size, that line becomes blurry and we fall back on old favorites regardless of whether they are stylish, are from high school, or even fit us. Our closets consist of the clothes we wear, the clothes we wish we could wear, the clothes we keep in case we gain weight or lose weight, and the clothes that someone told us we looked good while we were wearing it (I hear that one all the time). But after a while, our closets are full of so much CRAP we end up wearing the same thing by living out of our laundry baskets. Sound familiar?

If you need help deciding on what your individual style is as you get older, Kim Johnson Gross, author of *What to Wear for the Rest of Your Life* (2010) can help. Gross helps us discover our "closet identity" – the clothes that define us – and use that identity to reimagine who we want to be. The book is full of interviews with dozens of women and fashion advice on how to choose clothes for your shape, your lifestyle, and your current role in life. As you go through your closet and decide whether to keep or let go of each piece of clothing, ask yourself, "How long have I had this? Do I like it? Do I feel good in it? How often do I wear it? Is this the look I'm going for?"

All women deserve carefree closets because they make us feel good about our bodies no matter the size or shape. Clothing should be something we feel good wearing and our closets should be easy to navigate and maintain.

LET'S BREAK IT DOWN:
Sort first:

- Sorting is the only way to assess how much of each item you have.

- Pull everything out of your closet and sort by type of clothing. Sort items from drawers and dressers separately – one piece of furniture at a time.

- Categorize by type: short sleeve, long sleeve, pants, skirts, blazers, evening wear, etc.

- Begin to think quality over quantity.

Donate clothing if you haven't worn it for two years:

- If an item still has the tag on it, donate it, sell it on consignment (or eBay), or give it away. Keeping it doesn't justify the purchase. Donate it and forget it.

- Look on the Internet for women's career donation centers to donate office clothing. These women need your clothes to take the next step in their lives.

- Donate clothing if outdated. Surf the Internet for tips from fashion gurus such as Tim Gunn and Michael Kors. Read fashion magazines such as *Vogue* and *Elle* to find out what's in style each season. I love the magazine entitled *More* for tips on age-appropriate clothing styles.

New item in, old item out:

- When you bring in something new, let go of something you know you'll never wear again.

- When seasons end, only switch clothing meant exclusively for one season (e.g. wool items), not your whole closet. Wear basics all year 'round.

- Purge your wardrobe at the end of summer and winter. Let go of clothing you don't feel good in, is too small/big, is more than five years old, or is worn out, faded, pilly, or stained.

Concentrate on your current size:

- Watch the television show *What Not to Wear* for ideas on dressing for your body type.

- Keeping items that are too small makes you feel guilty.

- Keeping items that are larger allows you to go off your diet (I learned this from a client).

- Keep a few classic or expensive pieces in smaller and larger sizes just in case.

Underwear and lingerie:

- Replace stretched out or stained lingerie.

- Get a bra fitting (*I did and it changed the way I dressed!*).

- Wear comfortable underwear, not what looks good on other women.

- Keep different colors of pantyhose, leggings, or tights in separate clear zipper bags.

Jewelry:

- If you have to wade through your jewelry to find the piece you want, hand some down to relatives/friends, donate it, or sell it.

- Fine jewelry is always in style. Wear it often and not just for special occasions.

- Sentimental jewelry is always in style too, but if you have too much of it, keep your favorite pieces and let go of the rest.

- Sell old gold and silver jewelry you don't wear.

- Costume jewelry goes in and out of style – purge often.

Shoes:

- If shoes hurt or don't fit, donate them to thrift stores or send to www.Soles4Souls.com. This Nashville-based charity collects new and used shoes to support micro-business efforts to eradicate poverty.

- Repair or replace heels on good shoes. Replace sneakers often because arches break down.

- Place dryer sheets in shoes to keep fresh.

- Store shoes without boxes – this takes up less room and you are more likely to wear them. Keep good shoes you don't wear often in the box, take a picture of the shoes and tape it to the box.

- Store summer sandals vertically in a round basket – takes up less room and they are easier to find.

Belts and Scarves:

- Keep belts that fit and are in style. Purge the rest.

- Hang belts and scarves on wall hooks inside your closet or on a clothes rack. You'll be more likely to wear them. Use Command® hooks or get out your drill.

- Discover new ways to use scarves (e.g. tie onto a purse; use as a belt).

- Store small scarves flat in clear zipper bags with air pressed out. Takes up less room and you can see through the bag.

Sweatpants, t-shirts, work-out clothes:

- Keep the nicest and most memorable t-shirts.

- Don't use t-shirts and sweat pants as pajamas. You deserve real pajamas.

- Go through work-out clothes and eliminate stretched out or uncomfortable pieces – make sure you can move.

- Wear sweatpants made for women, not men.

Finishing touches:

- Categorize by color: Think Roy G. Biv (an acronym for the seven colors of the rainbow: red, orange, yellow, green, blue, indigo, violet)

- Have two types of hangers: fuzzy hangers for sweaters and sleeveless tops and smooth hangers for items you want to pull off the hanger and go. Recycle the wire ones at the dry cleaners.

Carefree closets don't make us feel bad about ourselves or hold out-of-style clothing from our past. Make friends with your closet again. Smile when you get ready in the morning. Donate your unneeded clothing to someone who would be happy to have it. Is there a carefree closet in your future?

SUCCESS IN ACTION

Sarah hadn't gone through her closet in 25 years and there were so many sizes in her closet she was overwhelmed. She fluctuated in weight and was afraid to let go of larger sizes in case she gained weight. She also had sentimental attachments to some pieces. We started by pulling everything out of the closet and only put back what was comfortable, was stylish, or qualified as a wardrobe staple. Sarah ended up taking ten garbage bags of clothing to the Goodwill Retail Store and made a list of items she needed to purchase to fill in the gaps. Now she shops with a purpose.

3.2

Is there a yard sale hiding in your attic?

"The things you own end up owning you."

quote from the movie *Fight Club*

If you have the average American attic or basement, it's probably filled with a lot of stuff (and CRAP). It doesn't matter whether you live in your home 10 or 50 years, it can be an overwhelming task to organize it or clean it out. If you are like many families, your attics and basements not only hold childhood memories, seasonal items, and old paperwork, they store items from parents, in-laws, aunts, or grandma when relatives move or pass away. The variety of items can be endless, and that's why most people don't clean out these rooms until they are ready to leave their home completely. The alternative is to leave it for the kids to worry about (*gasp!*).

> The variety of items can be endless, and that's why most people don't clean out these rooms until they are ready to leave their home completely.

Debbie Lillard, author of *Absolutely Organized: A Mom's Guide to a No-Stress Schedule and Clutter-Free Home* (2008) says that organizing is like dieting – "you can't do it fast and furious for two weeks and think you are done. You have to incorporate organizing into your daily life if you really want to change the way you are living." In other words, once you have finished cleaning out your attic or basement, you'll want to think before you put anything back into those spaces or you'll be cleaning the same space out again.

Clutter in attics and basements can cause a real burden – even embarrassment – to families. If you feel like your things own you and you've had enough, call on your family, friends, or a professional to set a date to start cleaning out. They will help and encourage you toward your goal of downsizing, donating, or finding treasures to sell at a yard sale or pass down to family members. You may be surprised how many unneeded items you have that would be useful to other people. Before those items deteriorate or become obsolete let them go.

LET'S BREAK IT DOWN:

Getting started on that overwhelming attic or basement:

- Set aside a full day to tackle your project. If that's not enough, schedule more days until you finish the job.

- Play your favorite music and wear comfortable clothing.

- Plan to order food in at the end of the day because you'll be too tired to cook.

- Call adult children and schedule a time for them to come and get their stuff (you are not a storage facility).

- If you are saving things for your children, ask them about it. Don't be offended if they tell you that your family heirlooms are not their taste. Pass it on to someone who will treasure, appreciate, and use it.

- Label every box you decide to keep. Mark contents on two sides of the box so you can store it in any direction.

Attics:

- If your attic is inconvenient or consists of a crawl space that gives you the creeps, you don't have to use it. It's okay to leave it empty.

- Do not keep photographs in hot attics – the pictures will be ruined by melting together.

- Store infrequently used items in your attic such as holiday and seasonal items, old tax records, and suitcases.

- Store items where they can't get wet from leaky roofs or open vents.

- Nothing precious belongs in your attic. If you love it or want to keep it, honor it by using it or incorporating it into your home. Otherwise, give it to someone who will use it.

- Cardboard boxes are fine for storage if areas are well-ventilated, dry, and critter-free – otherwise you're inviting pests. Invest in plastic containers with lids where needed.

Basements:

- Watch for water in unfinished or damp basements. Use plastic storage boxes with lids to keep items dry and safe from critters, mold, or mildew.

- Store boxes on shelves or pallets in unfinished basements.

- If you still have unpacked boxes from your last move (you know who you are), open each box and go through the contents before the items are obsolete or unusable. You could find items you thought you lost!

- Don't hold on to Grandma's furniture for more than two years waiting for someone to need it or to find a place to use it. Try not to feel guilty: you aren't getting rid of Grandma – just her stuff.

If there's a yard sale hiding in your attic, fear not! Don't let your CRAP own you – ask for help, hire a professional organizer or tackle it yourself with reckless abandon. Sell your stuff at a yard sale and use the money for your next vacation, a visit to the spa, or a new computer for the family.

SUCCESS IN ACTION

Jennifer's attic was full of her four grown children's memories such as trophies, sports memorabilia, and college textbooks. Her children lived in different parts of the country in their own homes, but every time they came to visit, they didn't want to take the time to go through their stuff. She hired me and we divided the attic into four sections and placed all the items for each child in those areas. She gave them all one month to come and get their belongings or she would dispose of it herself. She no longer wanted to be the storage facility for their stuff – and it worked!

3.3

Do you have a no-car garage?

"Order is never observed; it is disorder that attracts attention because it is awkward and intrusive."

Eliphas Levi, *French occult author and magician*

We didn't have a garage when my husband and I bought our house 28 years ago so when it came time to build one, we chose to build a detached two-story garage. I was amazed how quickly we filled it with stuff from the house, the basement, and the barn – items that really belonged in a garage in the first place. The second story was built specifically as a hangout for our son and his friends because his room was too small. The garage was far enough away from the adults, but close enough to the house so we could drop in on a moment's notice!

> Because you don't 'live' in the garage, it can become a clutter magnet: out of sight, out of mind.

Many families use garages as glorified storage facilities rather than a place for the car. Garages tend to become the dumping ground especially during the winter or when life is just plain busy. Because you don't 'live' in the garage, it can become a clutter magnet: out of sight, out of mind. "The average American two-car garage has become a no-car garage because it is crammed full of so much clutter," says Barry Izsak, author of the best-selling book, *Organize Your Garage in No Time* (2005). Izsak says that the biggest reason people struggle with garage organization is not because they can't do it, but because they are overwhelmed and don't know where to start.

The collection of stuff in any garage can range from overflow from the house, obsolete electronics, gardening supplies, unneeded building supplies, and a lot of stuff that doesn't have a home. As items build up, garages become awkward and sometimes dangerous to navigate. The best thing about organizing the garage is that if you do a really good job, it usually stays that way for a long time. Because the whole family probably uses the garage, bring everyone together and make it a family affair.

LET'S BREAK IT DOWN:
Start with a clean slate and unclutter:

- Pull **everything** out onto the driveway if you can (choose a fair weather day). Sweep it out by hand (or use a leaf blower or shop vacuum) and eliminate the cobwebs.

- Sort items by categories: lawn and gardening, work/tool bench, sports equipment, dry goods overflow, car accessories, power equipment, paints/solvents, lawn furniture, beach items, camping, etc.

- Talk to your children about their items and help them eliminate clutter (a.k.a. CRAP). Consider having a garage sale to sell their unused toys.

- Finish or let go of the supplies for unfinished projects and repairs (two years old or more).

- Find a new home for stuff that shouldn't be stored in an uninsulated garage (e.g. photographs, items that could melt or freeze).

- Eliminate duplicates and donate unneeded tools, doors, windows, or appliances to Habitat for Humanity ReStore. They sell items used to build homes and use the proceeds to build houses. Search the Internet for a store closest to you.

- Gather hazardous waste items (e.g. oil-based paint) for neighborhood cleanups. Call your township office to ask where and when you can dispose of these or if they collect them. Store them in a safe place away from children and pets until you dispose of them.

Type of storage/system:

- Put the largest items back into the garage first and set up shelving and other items around the largest items.

- Think 'up'. Store infrequently used items on high floating shelves, beams, or walls.

- Rest metal on wood or up on the wall on hooks. Metal on cement will rust.

- Pegboards work well on studs with no dry wall. Cut different sizes of pegboard according to the types of stuff and the space you have.

- Use open wire epoxy-coated steel shelving: wet things can dry and the mesh prevents dust.

- Consider a garage storage system: go to Lowe's, Home Depot, or a small business distributor in your area who specializes in garage systems. Tackle the installation yourself, invite a friend over to help, or hire a professional.

- Use different colored plastic bins for different zones so it's easier to put things away. Label everything. Don't make yourself guess what's stored in your bins.

- Hang long things vertically so they take up less space (e.g. garden rake, shovels). Drill a hole in the handle if it doesn't have one, tie a cord on the end and hang.

- Remix things you may already own and use for storage: old kitchen drawers/cabinets, a multi-shoe storage bag on the wall to hold small garden tools, or an old kitchen table as a work bench, etc.

Stay in the Zone:

- Divide the garage into zones according to the categories you've established from the list above.

- Think 'grab and go' and store things where they are convenient.

- Hang tools where they are most accessible.

- Keep car accessories close to the cars.

- Store overflow from the kitchen close to the door to or near the house.

- Reposition some zones as the seasons fluctuate: move bikes, beach items and lawn furniture down in spring and move the skis and sleds up high.

When our garages are organized, we can park our cars without difficulty and go in and out with ease. If you enter your home through the garage, hang a welcome sign, clean the door, and place a nice door mat on the floor. You deserve a nice welcome home after a long day's work!

SUCCESS IN ACTION

I got a call from Doug who was frustrated with his garage because it wasn't flowing the way he had hoped. When his family moved into the house, the boxes for the garages were just placed unopened on the floor in no special order. After asking him a lot of questions about his goals, future projects, and family use of the garage, we divided the garage into zones. With his brawn and my brains, we had a two-car garage organized in half a day. He especially loved the area we set up to hang out with his buddies: it included a few bar stools, a small refrigerator, and a small television.

3.4

A kitchen is a personal thing

"Cooking is like love,
it should be entered into with abandon or not at all."

Harriet Van Horne, *critic and columnist*

Before we put an addition on our house, it took me two years to research what I wanted in my new kitchen. Space and funds were limited so planning was important. I'm the kind of person who loves the process as much as the result – and a kitchen is such a personal thing. Whether you love to cook or not, a kitchen is a reflection of your personal lifestyle. Before our new kitchen, meal time was a hassle and a distraction because it was laid out poorly and there wasn't much cabinet space (I affectionately called our old kitchen the galley of the Mayflower.). After our new kitchen, I enjoyed cooking and ended up spending more time with my husband and son preparing and eating dinner. Maybe that's one of the reasons my son became a chef!

> You don't need a large kitchen for it to be well-equipped and organized.

There are so many good reasons to have an organized kitchen: you can eat healthier, cooking at home saves money, and teaching your children how to cook puts good habits in place for when they move out on their own. Peter Walsh said in his book *Enough Already! Clearing Mental Clutter to Become the Best You* (2009), "Good physical health comes from meals carefully chosen, lovingly prepared, and mindfully eaten." Walsh also says that when our kitchens are cluttered, preparing meals is a bother and we default to the easy choice which isn't necessarily the healthiest choice.

Whether your kitchen is a galley or a chef's dream, it tends to be the hub of the home. But even a small kitchen can flow easily if you have the right equipment in the right places. You don't need a large kitchen for it to be well-equipped and organized. Cooking macaroni and cheese or a gourmet meal is easier to make in an organized kitchen. In addition, groceries can be put away in a snap and cleanup is a breeze. Nowhere else in the home reaps such large rewards from your organizing efforts.

LET'S BREAK IT DOWN:
Kitchen Basics:

- Organize the three main centers of activity in your kitchen to form a triangle: stove, sink, and refrigerator.

- Have Rachael Ray's (Food Network personality) five kitchen basics close at hand: a good sharp knife, a huge cutting board with rubber feet, a big deep sided skillet, a good wooden spoon, and a bowl for garbage kept by the cutting board. Go to her website for quick and easy recipes at www.rachaelray.com.

- Keep daily-use items on the counter. Seasonal and least-used items can go up high in the cabinets.

- Chop and freeze frequently used foods such as onions, lemons, limes, basil leaves in olive oil, green/red/yellow peppers, etc. Routine chopping is something I enjoy to slow me down and is even better with my under-the-cabinet kitchen television in view.

- Choose good lighting for working on counters and for ambiance.

- Reorganize your kitchen as your family grows.

Cabinets:

- Take everything out of each cabinet, clean the shelves, and install fresh shelf paper (if necessary).

- As you organize, ask yourself "Did I use this item in the past year, how often did I use it, and how was the item used?" This will determine if you keep it and where you'll place it.

- Group items by category: mugs, drinking glasses, wine glasses, etc. If you have too much of one type, donate the excess.

- Keep one layer of items (e.g. mugs and glasses) to avoid breakage. Learn to resist the free glasses and travel mugs at gas stations and restaurants if your cabinets are already stuffed full.

- Show items that are attractive through glass cabinet doors.

- Use the back of cabinet doors to hang shelving for spices, canned food, bags for recycling, etc.

- Keep similar sizes of plastic food containers: store lids and bottoms separately, and resist the urge to have every size and shape.

- Use quality pots and pans and keep only what you really use (about 6-7 pieces).

- Hang frequently used items such as measuring spoons and cups under cabinets with tea cup hooks.

Counter tops:

- Keep counter tops clear for maximum work space.

- Keep only daily-use appliances, utensils, and food on the counter.

- Keep a cutting board with rubber feet on the counter so it's ready to use. Store vertical if space is at a premium.

- Use an under-the-cabinet television/DVD/CD or iPod/ iPhone speakers to save counter space and encourage meal preparation.

- Hang pot holders and frequently used towels on walls or drawers to save counter space.

Kitchen Drawers:

- Keep silverware in a drawer organizer. I store my sharp knives under my drawer organizer in their own open storage container.

- Go through the gadget drawer and question the use of each item and decide if you need to keep it. Use small containers to group similar items such as corn-on-the-cob holders and snack bag clips.

- Sharpen knives that don't cut or throw them away. Keep a few in a wood block on the counter that you use daily.

- For a quick and inexpensive kitchen makeover, replace the old cabinet knobs and drawer pulls with new ones.

Pantry:

- Use graduated shelving so you can see every item.

- Go through food frequently and eliminate outdated items. Donate the excess to a food pantry in your area.

- Store large or heavy items on the floor and infrequently used items on top shelves.

- Store light weight items on the top shelves and have a step stool nearby to kick around as you need it – my kitchen has cabinets that go to the ceiling so I use a small Rubbermaid® stool every day.

- Store inventory or overflow from the kitchen at the bottom of the basement steps or right outside the door to the garage.

Finally, remember to use the 'good stuff' everyday – the pretty tea cups for tea and the best crystal for wine. The good stuff really is meant to be used – besides what are you saving it for? You are the most important person in your house and just as good as company (*I learned this from one of my clients*)!

SUCCESS IN ACTION

Jill had two young children and worked full-time. Her kitchen was a source of frustration, and putting away groceries was inconvenient and difficult. Also, because she was Jewish she wanted to have kosher areas set up. She contacted me and we first got to work by going through each kitchen cabinet and talking about how and if each item was used. We let go of a lot of plastic containers she wasn't using, narrowed down the pots and pans, and cleared off the center island. We set up separate areas for kosher and non-kosher items. Now that the kitchen is organized, she said putting away her groceries is easy and her children can help.

3.5

Bathrooms: Shrines to the cosmetics industry

"Elegance is refusal."

Diana Vreeland, *fashion columnist and editor*

My upstairs bathroom is very small in my old farm house. There's barely enough room to dry off, but I make it work. Luckily, I don't have to share the bathroom with my husband because he has his own bathroom downstairs – my bathroom may be little, but it's all mine. I'm not a morning person so I have very few toiletries on the counter because too many choices annoy me.

> Bathrooms are our hiding places, our sanctuary away from the phone, children, and significant others.

In my experience as an organizer, the average bathroom has 299 different beauty products and toiletries in it (just kidding), but nowhere in the home is the number of choices and the cosmetic industry's influence more apparent than in the bathroom. Their advertising is meant to send a message that we are not good enough, not young enough, and not beautiful enough. We fill our bathrooms with promises of a more beautiful self and often don't think of what is in these products. The Campaign for Safe Cosmetics (www.SafeCosmetics.org) is a coalition effort launched in 2004 to protect the health of consumers and workers by working to eliminate dangerous chemicals from cosmetics and personal care products. In other words, they are making sure we aren't poisoned by our beauty and bath products. I found out my anti-bacterial soap has a pesticide as its main ingredient!

The bathroom should be a place you can have a quiet moment alone: even if it's only five minutes. Bathrooms are our hiding places, our sanctuary away from the phone, children, pets, and significant others. Having a simplified, organized bathroom without clutter and toxic products will give you peace of mind and help you relax when you get ready in the morning and go to bed at night.

LET'S BREAK IT DOWN:
Bathroom Basics:

- Good lighting, high wattage. Magnifying mirrors for the visually challenged (*like me*).

- Big trash can. It can be pretty, but make it big enough so it doesn't overflow.

- Keep only things you use every day on the counter or sink. All other items go in the medicine cabinet, underneath the sink, or in the linen closet.

- Use a shower caddy over the shower head or a corner shelf in the stall. Think 'up' – get things off the tub for safety reasons and easier cleaning.

- Have enough towel rods for everyone using the bathroom or have hooks in kid's rooms to hang wet towels (hang at child height).

- Buy a fabric hotel shower liner. It is an affordable luxury and you can wash and reuse it.

- Designate a place for everything and make it easy to put things away.

Bath and beauty products:

- Go to www.SafeCosmetics.org and find out what's really in your products.

- Keep one container or drawer of make-up. Throw out make-up that is old or never lived up to its hype (a.k.a. CRAP). Keep spare items in a container in the linen closet or out of the way. Resist the 'free' gifts at the cosmetics counter. They encourage you to buy things you don't need.

- Limit kid's bath toys to one bucket.

- Keep one type of each product and daily-use items (e.g. shampoo, moisturizer) in the bathroom. Store overflow in another location.

Medications:

- Dispose of expired medications, prescription medicines, or products that don't work as promised. This includes pills, ointments, cough liquids, sunscreens, etc. Ask your pharmacist where you should dispose of them.

- Clean out toiletries you haven't used or don't want and give them to homeless shelters (including those little bottles from hotels).

- Store like items together in separate containers, e.g. make-up brushes, Q-tips®, cotton balls, nail polishing items, etc.

Linens and Towels:

- Fold towels in sets (bath, hand, wash) for easy storage and retrieval. When towels are worn out, take to an animal shelter for use as bedding.

- Store bed linen sets inside one of the pillowcases for easy retrieval – no more hunting through piles for a match.

- Keep cleaning supplies in a tote for easy retrieval – preferably up high and away from children and pets. Keep one of each type of product in the tote. Store overflow separately.

- If fitted sheets lose their elasticity, make extra pillow cases out of the fabric (*yes, I've done this*) or donate the sheets to the homeless shelter.

Look around your bathroom and talk to yourself about what you see. Are you easily influenced by advertisements for the next best product that will change your life? Giving yourself too many choices in the bathroom is not freedom: it debilitates you. Trust your judgment, get informed, and refuse to buy into the hype.

SUCCESS IN ACTION

Lem had a large bathroom filled with every imaginable bath and beauty product. She wanted a calmer start to her morning when getting ready for work – she also had children to get off to school. We started by pulling all the products together (including the items she stored in her linen closet) and sorted into categories, e.g. shampoo, conditioner, body wash, cleaning supplies, etc. We donated the excess to the women's shelter. We put the remaining items into containers that fit on the shelves and narrowed down the number of items she placed on her bathroom counter. Mornings are now less stressful – no more CRAP to wade through!

CHAPTER 4

An Organized Office is No Place for CRAP

Owning a filing cabinet doesn't make you organized, any more than owning a cookbook makes you a chef.

4.1

Paper: The bad boy of the clutter family

*"It is estimated that 80% of paper filed away
is never looked at again."*

Small Business Administration

I'm going to go out on a limb and say that paper is the worst kind of clutter – many of my clients would agree. (That's why this book is also available electronically.) In the first place, paper clutter comes in the front door by way of the mailbox without any effort on your part. In the second place, it's just not easy to decide what to keep and what not to keep, so the decision is delayed and you end up keeping more than you should. Many of my clients also struggle between wanting to read what comes in the door and not having the time. So it piles up and up and out and well, you get the idea.

On the other hand, we generate our own paper at home and at work by printing e-mails and Internet information. Here are some 'fun' facts about paper:

- The average American uses more than 748 pounds of paper per year[3].

- The United States uses approximately 68 million trees each year to produce 17 billion catalogues and 65 billion pieces of direct mail[4].

- Approximately 85 gallons of water is used to produce 2.2 pounds of paper[5].

These kinds of facts make me want to stop printing anything. I started recycling my junk mail when I started my business and I was appalled at the amount of paper I used to throw in the trash (*shame on me*). Generally only 20% of the mail you receive is worth opening. Much of your mail is meant to sell you something you don't want, can't afford, or don't need. So for the 80% you didn't request (a.k.a. CRAP), don't feel compelled to open it and for heaven sake, don't keep it around. Recycle it or better yet, stop it from coming. Controlling mail and paper clutter isn't as hard as it seems.

> Much of your mail is meant to sell you something you don't want, can't afford, or don't need.

LET'S BREAK IT DOWN:
Tips to reduce your mail:

- First, set up a system to eliminate what's currently coming through the door.

- Transition to paperless statements for your bills and bank statements.

- Decrease the amount of national advertising mail you receive by logging on to the websites below. You can opt out of receiving pre-screened credit and insurance offers, get your name off e-mail lists, and remove deceased individual names from marketing lists.

  - www.obviously.com/junkmail

  - www.41pounds.org

  - www.optoutprescreen.com

  - www.catalogchoice.org

- If your reading folder/basket gives you more angst than pleasure, start to reduce it by cancelling at least one publication to which you currently subscribe or recycle anything older than three months.

- Many magazines, newspapers, newsletters, and association publications are available online. If and when you want to read it, you can go to the website or download to your Kindle, smartphone, iPad, or Nook.

Backlog of paper:

- Set aside a few hours each week and chip away at it. Remember that you can get most information online so you don't need to keep the paper around.

- Set up an area on a clear surface or table and sort paper into categories – like with like.

- If it took years to accumulate your paper, be patient with yourself to eliminate it. If you thought it was so important to keep it, take the time to look through it and convince yourself you will never keep this much paper again.

- If there are some papers you just cannot part with, consider scanning them into your computer, e.g. recipes, cards from friends, etc.

Snail mail:

- Stop it at the door! Keep a trash can, recycling bin, or shredder close to where you open your mail.

- Immediately rip up or shred credit card offers, junk mail, unrequested solicitations, etc.

- Discard old catalogs when a new one comes: keep your catalogs in one place alphabetically – easier to find, easier to discard.

- Place bills where you pay them (e.g. on the desk, at the computer, basket on the kitchen table, etc.).

- Don't keep the opened envelopes. Unfold all papers – this takes up less room when filing.

- Place important papers to keep (taxes, insurance, annuities, etc.) in **one** place and file once a month. See Chapter 4.2 for a simplified filing system.

- Keep invitations, things to take care of without delay, and calls to be made, etc. in **one** place, preferably where you pay bills so you are more likely to complete the task on a regular basis.

- Put magazines and other mail you want to read into a reading folder/briefcase (for reading on the go) or basket/box (for home reading).

To shred or not to shred:

- It's not necessary to shred something just because it has your address on it. Anyone can get your address from the Internet: it's public information.

- Shred papers that contain social security numbers, credit card numbers, open bank account numbers, credit card offers with your name on it, current annuity information, and personal medical information.

- Goodwill Retails Stores and Office Max will shred in bulk for a minimal cost. Many companies offer their employees shredding in bulk or burning paper.

- Look in the local paper or ask your local bank for free shredding events especially around tax filing time.

- Ask your tax accountant or financial planner for advice on what papers to keep and how long.

Recycle your paper and junk mail:

- If your town doesn't pick up paper to recycle, search the Yellow Pages book or website or go online and find a recycling center in your area.

- Abitibi-Consolidated is among the largest paper recyclers in North America. Paper Retriever® bins are located at thousands of collection points. Visit them at www. PaperRetriever.com to find a bin closest to you.

If you're dealing with a backlog of paper, perseverance is critical. Ask yourself, "Will I have the time or take the time to read this? Will I suffer irreparable harm if I throw this away? Is my paper causing me more pain than pleasure?" After that, be future-oriented: only keep the paper that you absolutely need, want, or must keep for your future goals.

SUCCESS IN ACTION

Matthew and Avery had three small children and no time to organize their paper files and the children's papers from school. After gathering the backlog of the paperwork into one room, we sorted and purged. We moved some furniture around to accommodate a mail sorting station for the future influx of paper from snail mail, work-related paper, and schools (big tree-killers). The hardest part of organizing a backlog of paper is to stick with the process. These clients were motivated and focused so the outcome was a success.

4.2

Filing system simplified

"Indecision is fatal. It is better to make a wrong decision than build up a habit of indecision."

Marie Beynon Ray, *American author*

If paper organization is a challenge for you, you are not alone. Take my husband: he insists that any of his important papers have to be out in his view. That's the reason why our kitchen table is also his desk – the kitchen is the hub of the home, so that's where his paper is. About once a month, I 'help' him go through the paper to find a home for some of it, throw some away, and keep the rest lying out. The best I can hope for is that his papers stay in an organized pile and there's room to eat a meal.

> If paper organization is a challenge for you, you are not alone.

In Julie Morgenstern's book *Organizing from the Inside Out* (1998), there's a whole chapter on what holds us back from organizing our homes and that bad boy of clutter – paper. Between the psychological obstacles, external realities and fear of getting it wrong, no wonder we freeze when it comes to devising the perfect filing system. The main motivation to organizing paper is to find what you need when you need it. When you can't find what you need, bills get paid late, late fees are incurred, and your credit rating could suffer. And here's the biggest dilemma: when it comes to paper, everyone's filing system for finding what they need is different. It can take years of trial and error to find the best way to organize your paper.

Thankfully, many banks, utility companies and department stores are offering paperless statements. I go paperless whenever it's offered. If you want to look at your bank statement from January 2009, you go to the computer, not the box in the attic. However no amount of paperless banking will take the responsibility away from us to keep certain documents for Uncle Sam and other entities. There is plenty of software to assist you when setting up a paper filing system or a digital filing system, but uncomplicated is best.

The following is a system that can be the basis for any personal filing system. Your system will differ in subtle ways – but keep it simple. The more categories you have, the longer it will take you to find what you need. If you have a small business, keep those files in a separate area.

LET'S BREAK IT DOWN:

Set up one folder for each of the following in alphabetical order:

Bank Accounts

- Each checking account

- Each savings account

- Credit reports – request one yearly at tax time to keep track of your credit rating. Go to www.annualcreditreport.com or www.creditkarma.com.

- Safe deposit box contents

Car

- One file for each car-repairs and warranties

- AAA, State car registrations, EZ-Pass information

Credit Cards

- Banks
- Department stores and others

Home

- Property information
- Mortgage
- Home equity loan
- Township information
- Inside/outside home improvements
- Decorating ideas
- Receipts for large home purchases

Insurance

- Car
- Fire
- Life

Medical

- Insurance-current year expenses and explanation of benefits
- Blank medical forms and coverage information
- Medical file for each family member-test results, etc.

Miscellaneous

- Everybody has one – keep it small.
- If there is more than three pieces of paper about the same thing, make its own folder.

Pet Information

Retirement

- Each company/annuity
- Social Security

Taxes

- Current year
- Last year (keep all prior years in another location-seven years maximum)

Utilities

- Gas/Oil
- All phones
- Electric
- Cable

Warranties (I keep these in our attic because I don't use them often)

- Large appliances
- Small appliances

- Large electronics

- Small electronics

- Inside the home-miscellaneous

- Outside the home-miscellaneous

Maintenance is the key:

1. Keep papers 'to file' in **one** basket close to the filing cabinet. Filing every day is unrealistic.

2. Do your filing when the papers get as high as the bin or basket (My own basket is 2" high so I file when it hits the top.)

3. Find a comfy chair, pour your favorite drink, put in a good movie, and file.

Filing help:

- Three paper organization websites: www.freedomfiler.com, www.thepapertiger.com, and www.shoeboxed.com.

- Smartphone app *OfficeDrop*-scan, search, organize and store your paper files

- NeatReceipts or NeatDesk-portable scanner and digital filing system

- Go to the Wells Fargo website at www.wellsfargo.com[6] for a list of papers keep and what to throw out.

Bottom line: If it has an impact on your taxes or is needed for legal, insurance, or warranty reasons, keep it. If you still own it, e.g. annuity, home, car, keep the paper. If you must keep the paper, but don't look at the file at least once a month, take it to the attic or basement. Indecision leads to piles of paper and not being able to locate important documents when you need them. No filing system is perfect. Make the decision to keep or not to keep and change your system as needed – trust your judgment.

SUCCESS IN ACTION

After his wife passed away, Mason called me because he was lost in a sea of paperwork. His wife was ill for many years and she had been in charge of bill paying and paper organization – things had gotten out of hand. We started by shredding and recycling the old paperwork that was getting in his way. Next we secured the most recent tax returns and put them in a safe place. Finally, we sorted the remainder of his important papers to determine what he wanted to keep and filed them in a simple file box. We set up a filing system to keep track of current and incoming paperwork. Mason finally felt he had a handle on his sea of paper.

4.3

Technology – Individual as a thumbprint

"In the year 3000, YouTube, Twitter, and Facebook will combine to create one huge time wasting device called UTwitFace."

Conan O'Brien, *comedian*

After many months, my iPhone and I have finally bonded. It was touch and go for a while because my son (a.k.a. my personal Geek Squad) wasn't around to talk me through it when I got frustrated – but now it's my virtual assistant. I've eliminated the phone number section of my week-at-a-glance day planner and added them to my iPhone (*that was a big step for me*). I love technology, as long as I can program it to work **for** me and not **against** me. I'm always willing to change if it's to my benefit. The combination of an iPhone for contacts and a day planner for making appointments works for me – for now.

Personal technology is like a thumbprint – as different as each individual. When my clients ask me what type of day planner or time management device they should buy to stay better organized, I always have a lot of questions to ask before we arrive at an answer (see those questions below). Buying a new iPhone isn't going to make you an organized person just as buying a guitar doesn't make you Eric Clapton. In her eBook, *Taming the Paper Tiger in the Digital Age @ Home* (2011), Barbara Hemphill says that choosing the

> Buying a new iPhone isn't going to make you an organized person just as buying a guitar doesn't make you Eric Clapton.

right combination of technology is the key and she reminds us that there are no 'perfect' calendars; so many people use a combination. Busy families will also need a master calendar (e.g. posted in the kitchen) to coordinate schedules.

After you choose the right technology for you, learn how to use your device so it doesn't waste your time. I am a big proponent of reading the manual (gasp!) or going to a class to discover all the extra features your technology has to offer you. It's surprising how many people will tolerate aggravation from an inanimate object (e.g. allowing a phone call to interrupt your dinner when you have voice mail). Organize your technology to save time and frustration.

LET'S BREAK IT DOWN:

Choose the right time management device:

- Do you prefer electronic or paper or both (*like me*)? Choose what works for you and how you live. Don't feel pressured by advertising or others to pick one over the other.

- Do you miss appointments and special days? If so, use technology to get visual and audio reminders for these and other important events. I use www.SendOutCards. com to get e-mails to remind me of birthdays so I can send a card and a gift without leaving my home.

- Do you pay bills late? Use the smartphone apps *Mint.com* or *Pageonce* to track, control, and pay bills on time.

- Do you need to synchronize with an electronic calendar? Many employers require that you keep a specific type of calendar (e.g. Outlook) up-to-date even though you may have your own electronic or paper calendar.

- Do you need to see day, week, or month at a glance? I prefer weekly, but many people prefer a combination of weekly and monthly.

- Do you need task lists with your calendar? Make sure there's room on the calendar for making lists of daily tasks. I use week-at-a-glance and list tasks on the left and appointments on the right.

- Do you write down reminders in the car? I use the Voice Memos on my iPhone so I can keep my hands on the wheel.

Cellular Phone/smartphone/PDA:

- Choose a smartphone if you use your phone for business use, especially if you need 24/7 access to the Internet and e-mail.

- Go to a class, go online, or ask a savvy teenager for instructions on what your phone can do for you to stay organized. Program your phone to personalize it. Don't settle for default settings.

- Review contact list, pictures, and videos often and delete to make room for what you really want and need. Anything else is clutter (a.k.a. CRAP).

- Screen your calls and use voice mail. Don't allow interruptions if you are busy. Be the master of your domain (and your phone!).

- Use the contact categories for as much or as little information as you need to keep for each individual. Don't feel the need to add information you'll never use.

- Regularly delete your recent message and call logs, text logs, voicemail, etc. Send any important pictures to your computer for storage.

- Download only the apps you really want and need. Ask yourself if this app will help you stay organized and will it add value to your life or just clutter.

Computer organization:

- Organize your documents – Word, Excel, Publisher, and PowerPoint – into file folders.

- Categorize by project, organization, family member, etc.

- Unclutter your desktop. Keep only regularly used files on your desktop – not every file.

- Purge or reorganize files at least once a year (I do this at tax time).

- Attach dates to the name of the file if pertinent.

- Have a back-up system available so data is safe from a computer crash, especially if you work from home or have no technology department to call (*like me!*).

E-mail etiquette – KISS (Keep It Simple Son):

- Set your Internet options to hold a certain amount of history and temporary Internet files.

- Turn off the arrival bell or pop up: Answer e-mails on **your** time schedule.

- Use filters to limit what comes into your inbox every day.

- Respond within 24 hours (just a guideline). Immediate is not always necessary.

- Clean out inbox, sent mail, and deleted mail regularly or use settings to do it for you. Your goal should be an empty inbox (no, really).

- Organize e-mail messages into virtual folders or print out (if you must!) and keep in a temporary file folder on your desk to act upon later.

- Use a signature line to save time typing repetitive information such as your phone number or address. This was helpful when I changed my phone number.

- Use a detailed vacation reply when away, or when you are working on a large project and don't want to be disturbed. Don't forget to set an end date.

- For great tips to manage e-mail, read the book *Inbox Detox and the Habit of E-Mail Excellence* (2008) by Marsha Egan (or download the eBook version-2011).

Technology changes faster than we change our minds. Personalize your technology and use it to honor yourself and your time – it's a precious commodity. Upgrade to the next model when **you** are ready, and utilize it to its fullest extent to benefit you, your family, and your way of life.

SUCCESS IN ACTION

My husband has a technology phobia – he gets frustrated just using a copier. So when my husband wanted a new cell phone, he took our son with him to help choose the right phone. My son gave my husband a tutorial on the new phone and asked lots of questions to learn how my husband wanted and needed to use the phone. Not only did my husband learn how to text, but now he uses his cell phone to retrieve and answer e-mails. He may actually learn to like technology!

4.4

Death, taxes, and a line at Starbucks

"If you think getting organized is time consuming, try disorganization."

Jeff Davidson, *time management expert*

There are only two things for sure in this world: death and taxes. I added a line at Starbucks because it's true. Preparing your taxes can be intimidating, but a little organization during the year is the key. Being organized can help you do your taxes early to see if you're getting a refund or if you owe money. If it's the former, file early. If it's the latter, file and pay in early April. Never file last minute, especially if you are filing online for the first time – it always takes longer than you think (*been there, done that, paid the penalty*).

> Anything that makes the tax filing process easier, more efficient, and less error-prone is a good thing.

I used to work in a college financial aid office where we looked at tax returns every day so I was familiar with the ins and outs of a standard return. I am the financial person in our household so my husband knows that if anything happens to me, he'll need to call our accountant – or marry one! However, when my husband retired and I started my business, it became apparent I needed assistance from an expert. If you need an expert, call an accountant or go to H&R Block online. They have a user-friendly website at www.hrblock.com for just about any tax filer. They provide step-by-step guidance at whatever level you need and some of the advice is free. If online isn't your preference, go to any H&R Block location near you.

Finally, use as much technology as you can to file your taxes. Anything that makes the tax filing process easier, more efficient, and less error-prone is a good thing. I use Microsoft Excel for my business, because it meets my needs. If you need financial software for your business or personal use, ask friends and colleagues what works for them and assess your needs from there. New software to file taxes online will require copious amounts of patience so leave plenty of time so you don't miss the filing deadline.

Disclaimer: This information is not meant to be all-inclusive. Any questions should be directed to your tax accountant or www.irs.gov.

LET'S BREAK IT DOWN:
Getting organized to file taxes:

- Gather supplies: calculator, pencil with eraser, blank tablet, favorite snack, stapler, all receipts and paperwork, favorite drink, paper clips, computer, and tax return from the previous year.

- Purchase or download tax software early and choose the software that suits your needs or is compatible with software you already own. Don't overspend on something complicated if you don't need it.

- Gather all tax documents and files. Sort and organize these first before you attempt to enter your information onto the tax return or on the computer.

- Keep IRS websites on hand. For detailed information go to www.irs.ustreas.gov or to obtain forms and publications go to www.irs.ustreas.gov/prod/forms_pubs.

Donations and Deductions:

- Cash donations. You must have a receipt in order to deduct a cash donation: that means a cancelled check or statement from the charity. View *IRS Publication 526: Charitable Contributions*[7] online for guidance.

- Non-cash donations. For those of you who cleaned out clutter (and CRAP) and donated items last year, you will need to estimate fair market value for those donations. See *IRS Publication 561: Determining the Value of Donated Property*[8] online or go to Salvation Army website (www.salvationarmyusa.com), or Goodwill Industries website (www.yourgoodwill.org) for valuation lists.

- Car donations: You can only deduct what the nonprofit agency sold the car for, so ask for a receipt from the agency after your car is sold.

- Helpful resources: Some software programs calculate the fair market value of donated items for you (e.g. TurboTax). Smartphone users can download the apps *iDonatedIt* or *Donation* to organize donations.

Get organized for next year:

- Keep old tax returns out of the way in the attic or basement, and the most recently completed tax return easily accessible. Keep old electronic files on a separate flash drive or in an electronic folder under 'old taxes' by year. The IRS has up to three years from the due date of the return to audit your tax return. If the IRS finds an error and your tax is understated by 20% or more, they can go back seven years. If you aren't sure how long to keep other tax-related documents, get a copy of *IRS Publication 552: Recordkeeping for Individuals*[9].

• Develop a filing system that is simple and makes sense for you and your family; e.g. use color coding to separate personal and business. At the very least, keep a tax file folder to insert deductions, tax payments, and charity contributions during the year – preferably where you pay your bills or where you sort your mail. See Chapter 4.2 for tips.

• When you keep receipts for expenses, write what the charge was for on the receipt if it isn't obvious – otherwise you could forget (*I do!*). If you have a business, use the categories of expenses on IRS Schedule C. Go to www.irs.gov and click on forms and publications.

• If you write checks manually, document the purpose on the check register. Highlight cash donations on the check register so they are easier to spot at tax time.

• Check with your tax accountant in June to see if you should make any adjustments to deductions or withholding before the year is over.

Credit Reports:

• Check your credit report annually at tax time. For a free credit report and access to all three credit agencies, go to www.AnnualCreditReport.com or www.CreditKarma.com.

• For access to each credit agency go to: www.transunion.com, www.experian.com, or www.equifax.com. Or call: TransUnion (800) 916-8800; Experian (888) 397-3742; or Equifax (800) 685-1111.

- Ask your bank if they have a recent credit score on file for you. If you recently applied for a loan, they may have one available.

Take time to get organized to file taxes: being disorganized is aggravating and can cause sleepless nights. Planning ahead and having the necessary documents on hand gives you peace of mind. It can also save you money because it won't take your accountant or an H&R Block employee as long to complete your return!

SUCCESS IN ACTION

Don called me because he was overwhelmed with his paperwork. He kept his business and personal tax returns for as long as he'd been in business (20+ years). He was planning to move in the near future so before he did, he wanted to shed the unnecessary paper. We separated all the tax documents into piles: keep (most recent seven years), shred (anything older than seven years), and recycle (magazines and random paper). We also separated the personal and business tax returns into two different plastic bins and marked them. He was thrilled to see how little he would need to move to his new home.

4.5

Home-based business – A blessing and a challenge

"If you have an apple and I have an apple and we exchange these apples, then you and I will still each have one apple. But if you have an idea and I have an idea and we exchange these ideas, then each of us will have two ideas."

George Bernard Shaw, *Irish playwright*

Having a home-based business was never a dream of mine. I was convinced I needed to report to an employer every day to earn a living. I was wrong – because when you are passionate about what you do, your business becomes a labor of love. That said when I eliminated my land line phone in order to use my iPhone for business, it set up a ripple effect of changes that had to be made. As a result, I spent an entire morning crawling under my desk labeling the wires (with my label maker) to quickly identify my printer, lights, television, computer, phone, etc. (I really miss having a technology department to call when I worked for someone else.) Ah, the challenges of the home-based business.

> You can't be an expert at everything so rely on the expertise of other small professionals to enhance your business.

Starting a new business out of your home is exciting and intimidating. Whether you are baking cupcakes, designing websites, or doing taxes, you'll be drawing on many transferable skills from your other careers to run your business. But you can't be an expert at everything so rely on the expertise of other professionals to enhance your business. You'll find these talented people by joining the local chamber of commerce or joining a networking group. A barter network is another option for a home-based business or any type of small business. An article from the Wall Street Journal, *Let's Make a Deal: The growing role of barter in the marketplace*[10], advocates the benefits of corporate barter as a way to secure goods and services, move excess inventory, and attract new customers without laying out precious cash (see consider a barter network below).

Finally, when you operate a business out of your home, it can be too easy to operate in a vacuum and get caught up in your own world. Getting out into the public is crucial to sustain and build your business. In addition, anyone who operates a business from their home knows that staying focused can be a challenge. Keeping children, a spouse, and a few pets at bay is the additional ingredient that can add to the difficulty of concentrating (*I have two Jack Russells so I know from which I speak*). Here are a few of my tips for maximum profit and maximum focus.

LET'S BREAK IT DOWN:
Location, Location, Location:

- Secure a separate physical space for your office. This sounds like a no brainer, but you can't run a business from the corner of the bedroom or a nook in the kitchen.

- Set up an extra bedroom/guest bedroom as an office as long as you can close the door while working. When you're not working, doors help eliminate the temptation to work 24/7.

- Treat yourself and buy a comfortable office chair.

- Be creative with your office furniture – your office should be a reflection of yourself. Repurpose a Hoosier (antique kitchen furniture), a buffet (my favorite type of furniture for organization), or a wardrobe as office furniture. Buy from used office furniture stores for discounts on high-end furniture. I use a kitchen table from IKEA for a desk because it's a lot bigger than a typical desk.

- Think 'prime real estate' when you setup your desk. Keep everything you use on a daily basis at arm's length – or a chair scoot away (e.g. your phone, your current project or client files, the copier, certain office supplies, etc.)

Office Management:

- Hire a business coach or contact the Small Business Administration in your area for assistance. More knowledge is power.

- Develop the basic minimums before you begin your business: logo, tag line, business card, website, brochure/flier, 30-second elevator speech, and business plan.

- Develop marketing materials or have experts do it for you. Marketing professionals have expertise to help you and your business look good.

- Maximize your time and stay focused on your goals. If the task isn't goal-oriented – rethink it.

- Think efficiency and productivity. Time is money. If you aren't spending your time efficiently – rethink it (*confession: I play Spider Solitaire when I'm too tired to think*).

- Clean up and organize your desk once a week so it's easier to focus on current projects. You are your own boss so use whatever system works for you.

Consider a barter network:

- Barter networks (a.k.a. reciprocal trade, trade exchange) facilitate transactions and assist in tracking the revenue and expenses that must be reported for tax purposes.

- Provide your goods and services to clients within the barter network, receive credit for those services, and spend your credits with other businesses within the network.

- Find a barter network in your area or search the Internet for a national or international network to join.

- Obtain many items and services for free as a member of a barter network (e.g. graphic design services, eyeglasses, food at restaurants, printing, business coaching, etc.).

Don't operate in a vacuum:

- Network at least once a week to show the face behind your business (face to face or online).

- Join brainstorming, entrepreneur, mastermind, and coaching groups to help you build your business, exchange tricks of the trade, and keep your own ideas fresh. You can do these on the web or face-to-face.

- Get out of the house! Take your computer to restaurants, hotel lobbies, or local coffee shops with free Internet access. You are the face of your business so get out there and be seen – wear clothing with your logo on it.

- Take business reading in your car or answer e-mails on your smartphone to maximize time in between clients and errands (while parked of course).

- Offer to speak at organization meetings (e.g. Rotary, Lion's Club, ABWA-American Business Women's Association, and church groups) to get your business in front of the public's eye.

Finally, although having a home-based business gives you tremendous flexibility with your time, don't forget to schedule down time – or you'll never stop working. Being passionate about your business is great – just remember to stop and take time for fun.

SUCCESS IN ACTION

Mary Louise wanted to start an at-home eBay business, but didn't know how to get started. After selecting her finished basement as the ideal area for an office, we began to gather all the eBay items for sale (from all over the house) and all the packaging supplies into one area. As a result we relegated two shelving units, a dresser, and a small closet to house the items for sale and the packing supplies. We also set up an area for taking pictures and easy access to the computer. She was able to start selling items on eBay within one week.

CHAPTER 5

Families and their CRAP

Mazzei saved lots of money on spaghetti sauce, but it was the 5th night in a row for spaghetti and meatballs.

5.1

Selling your home? Clear the CRAP!

"Blessed are the flexible for they shall not be bent out of shape."

Michael McGriff, M.D., *American poet*

Any realtor will tell you that the first step to selling a house is to start to say goodbye to your home. When you decide to sell your house, you need to start looking at it through the eyes of a potential buyer. However, saying goodbye can be an emotional and difficult time in your life. 'Staging' a home to sell is a word realtors use to encourage sellers to depersonalize, unclutter, and simplify their homes. If you watch the television shows on HGTV about selling homes, you'll notice how inflexible some people are to changing their home in order to sell it. Memories are hard to pack away even if you are ready to sell.

> Clutter eats equity.

The second step to selling your home is to make a good first impression. Webb and Zackheim, authors of the book, *Dress Your House for Success* (1997) know what it takes to sell a home and that first impressions are critical. Getting buyers through the front door is half the battle – buyers must want to get out of their cars instead of just driving by. Buyers can develop an attitude toward your house within 15 seconds that is reinforced by everything else they encounter outside or inside your home. Your house will eventually sell: it's up to you to do whatever you can to get the best price.

The third and most critical step to selling your home faster and for top dollar is to remove the clutter. The number one home improvement that will give you 973% average return on your investment is cleaning and removing clutter[11]. Clutter eats equity. Clutter says this house is too small. First, let go of the CRAP and then gather the items you want to take with you and store them elsewhere to free up space. If I had to sell my small home tomorrow, I would have to remove half of the clutter (not CRAP) even though I like it the way it is. There are certain rooms that are most important to potential buyers and need the most attention, so here's some advice on 'staging' your home to sell.

LET'S BREAK IT DOWN:
Front door and porch (curb appeal means your house looks great from the curb before the buyer gets out of the car):

- Front door should sparkle or have fresh paint and a shiny door knob. This is an inexpensive fix with a big impact.

- Screen and storm doors should open easily.

- Add a spot of color with a wreath, planter, or bright decorative item.

- Porch should have new door mat, chairs, end table, and/ or plants.

- Mow the lawn. Trim shrubs. Do cursory gardening as needed (no dead plants).

- Keep lawn ornaments to a bare minimum. Remove any clutter on the lawn.

Entry Way (have one bold and dramatic focal point):

- Greet buyers with a 'welcome home' sign or wreath.

- Flowers are always a nice touch.

- Reduce furniture to make it easier to walk through and make rooms appear larger.

- Improve the floor: make repairs or replace if necessary.

- No loose throw rugs. One long rug is best.

- Clean out the coat closet. Place loose items in containers (gloves, hats, etc.).

Kitchen (your kitchen alone could sell your home):

- Clean off front and top of refrigerator and cabinets (no magnets or photos).

- Open a cookbook or display a bowl of fruit.

- Quick cabinet makeover: new knobs and/or hinges

- Clear counter of everything except a very few items.

- Create more storage if possible (e.g. rolling cart).

- Accent your windows: clean them and hang no curtains or choose curtains light in weight and color.

- Highlight a counter eat-in area if possible and use nice stools.

- Buy new towels/pot holders/dishcloths (you deserve new ones anyway).

- Clean out and organize what opens: cabinets, refrigerator, pantry, mop closet (stuffed cabinets mean your kitchen is too small).

Dining room or dining area (think 'family dinners'):

- Set the table with a few place settings, colorful placemats, glasses and utensils. Add a pretty centerpiece.

- Brighten the room with a pitcher of flowers, a candle or two, and a few plants.

- Multipurpose a large dining room: separate by adding a desk for paying bills, a chair for a reading nook, a music corner with a music stand, etc.

- Make a small dining area look larger: remove leaves in table, put table against the wall and remove extra chairs.

Living/family room (balance between casual and formal):

- Take down 90% of your family photos. Buyers want to imagine their family in the house, not yours.

- Pack away anything with 'eyes': stuffed animals, posters with people on them.

- Open curtains or eliminate them to bring in sunshine.

- Highlight fireplace mantel: spray paint screen, clean and unclutter mantel, and tastefully decorate.

- Remove excess clutter and furniture: widen exit and entry ways.

- Draw attention to exposed beams or cathedral ceilings with lighting, hanging basket, mobile, art, etc.

- Clean out what opens: cabinets, closets, built-ins, and toy chests.

- Add a few matching pillows and blankets for warmth.

- Organize bookshelves: organize books by size and leave white space: less is more.

- Organize electronics and accessories. Clean up wires.

- Gather papers and magazines after reducing and put into baskets or containers.

Finally, be as flexible as you can to make the changes necessary to sell your home. Have your carpets cleaned and have a professional clean your home top to bottom – clean sells. Getting your home ready to sell can be an exhausting process. However, everything you do to prepare is going to mean money in your pocket and bring you closer to a SOLD sign on your home. Good luck!

SUCCESS IN ACTION
Laurie had a very small home and needed to move to a larger home for her growing family. I helped her stage the home by removing half of the furniture in each room, converting a small sun room into an office, and uncluttering each room by packing up a lot of the décor. Her home was transformed to look spacious and uncluttered and she sold it for more than the asking price in one week.

5.2

Downsizing is not a four-letter word

"Use it up, wear it out, make it do, or do without."

saying from World War II

For some people, the word downsizing denotes a negative feeling because of businesses downsizing and laying off workers. But downsizing in the housing sense means moving from a large home to a smaller home and downscaling belongings at the same time. In his AARP article entitled *Conquering Clutter* (2007), David Dudley described downsizing his mom and dad's home as they prepared to move to a smaller home as a 'war'. He said it "was a clash, a struggle, a pitched battle with our stuff, and each other."

> It's difficult to part with things once loved but no longer needed.

I have worked with many clients who are ready to downsize. It's a struggle to make decisions and confusion about what to keep and let go of can set in quickly. Going through belongings can involve reliving 30, 40 sometimes 50 years of a life – a special coffee cup, a rocking chair that rocked babies, or a casserole dish that held grandma's famous stuffing. It's difficult to part with things once loved but no longer needed. Vickie Dellaquila, author of *Don't Toss My Memories in the Trash* (2007), says that it's usually best not to second-guess the parents' decisions on what to keep or not to keep. However, setting goals before the downsizing process begins is critical so everyone is on the same page and knows how much has to go.

When you help your parents downsize, they might feel you are trying to disregard the importance of their life and the things that went with it. Sensitivity is the key. If possible, downsizing should involve the whole family; even though many siblings live apart – sometimes it's up to one child. Planning ahead can help avoid any unpleasantness surrounding this inevitable task. Uncluttering at a feverish pace is not pleasant for anyone and can be devastating for the homeowner.

It's ideal to downsize when your parents aren't forced to leave in a hurry. Here's why:

- Any child who has cleaned out the house of a parent who has passed away can tell you it's exhausting.

- Choosing where to donate unneeded items is a desirable position compared to many people who don't have the choice of how to dispose of their belongings.

- When homeowners are physically able to help with the process and decide what goes with them, it can be mentally affirming and can offer a sense of control.

- Family stories about certain belongings can be a part of the process (e.g. "Grandma gave us this dish for a wedding present.").

- When a family member is no longer mobile or having health issues, throwing things out for them can make the owners feel violated.

- Clutter in the home is an obstacle course for people with limited mobility and can be dangerous.

When it's time to start downsizing your parent's belongings, everything suddenly seems precious. But the reality is that many things have to go and that fact can be hard to face.

Knowing that every family has its own dynamics, here are some ways to proceed:

- Discuss the plan to downsize with your parents and find out what seems equitable to them.

- Make the process a family affair. Not everyone has to participate if it's too difficult for some.

- Suggest that your parents begin the downsizing process at a family gathering. Your parents might ask relatives to privately pick out several things in the home they would like to have when your parents are ready to part with the items (some families use colored stickers).

- Ask your parents to begin giving these selected items as presents for birthdays, holidays, and wedding gifts to relatives and friends.

Finally, downsizing is an appropriate time to talk about sensitive information you need from your parents. Besides having lots of patience, here are some tips:

- Start the conversation like this: "I know I won't need this information for a long time, but I'd feel better if I knew what to expect."

- Know the location of their will, if it's current or needs updated, and the lawyer who drew it up. A copy should be with the executor.

- Know any Do Not Resuscitate (DNR) orders and other end-of-life directives.

- Find out if your parents are organ donors.

- Know the location of military discharge papers for military burial if they wish.

- Locate insurance policies, bank accounts, and the key to the safe deposit box.

- Ask about any hiding places for money and valuables (or have them write the locations down and put that paper in the safe deposit box).

If you have a parent who wants to begin downsizing, do everything you can to assist them. When parents want to take control of the process and want help to decide where they should donate or take their unwanted items, it's a good thing. Downsizing is hard work, but you'll be glad your parents initiated the process – it's a gift to you.

SUCCESS IN ACTION

Craig was in his 70's and decided that living five states away from his grown children was not where he wanted to live as he aged. He decided to move closer to his children and into a senior living center. His children hired me to assist him with the entire moving process. I located a moving company that was personable and could explain the process to him. We decided together what he would take with him and what to leave behind to donate and sell. After the move, Craig's son e-mailed me and said his dad was the happiest he'd seen him in a long time. He was making friends, going to the movies, and listening to live music. The facility where his dad lives takes him to appointments, the grocery store, and the bank – he no longer worries about his dad driving. That's what I call a win-win situation.

5.3
Moving – An opportunity in disguise

*"A plan without action is a daydream;
action without a plan is a nightmare."*

Japanese proverb

My husband and I have only moved once in our married life (30 years and counting), and I'm not looking forward to our next move because my husband doesn't fully grasp the concept of downsizing (he's a saver). Some of my clients are in that same position because they have lived in their homes for a long period of time and have never had to face moving their belongings. Other clients have moved often, but haven't taken the time to downsize before the move and have unopened boxes packed away for years. Moving is a challenging and stressful time, but it can be an opportunity to simplify and focus on what's really important to you and your family. Moving is also one of those events where you want to have an action plan or suffer the consequences.

> Moving is a challenging and stressful time, but it can be an opportunity to simplify and focus on what's really important to you and your family.

American Moving and Storage Association has a great website (www.moving.org) with a plethora of information on what to do before you move, how to hire a professional mover, and what happens after the move. Why leave it all to chance? One of my clients was moving across the country, so when we packed for her move, she eliminated anything that wasn't precious or replaceable.

Paying to transport items you don't need, don't want, or can easily replace (without a large layout of money) doesn't make sense – you're paying by the pound to move it.

When clients hire me to help them prepare to move, we create a game plan and map out what has to be done. If they don't have a moving company, I recommend one that I trust, even if they are only moving across town. The advantages of hiring a mover, even if it's a short distance away, can take a lot of stress off of the family. We talk a lot about purging because so many people are tired of their CRAP and want to take this opportunity to leave it behind. We decide what to donate, where to take those unneeded items, what to sell on eBay, and what is necessary or precious enough to make the cut and take to the next home.

LET'S BREAK IT DOWN:

Before a move (start at least six months before you move):

- File a change of address form with your local post office or online at www.moversguide.usps.com.

- Use your e-mail address book, smartphone contacts, and Facebook friends to notify friends and family of your new address. If you have an address book or Excel list of additional names and addresses for people who don't have electronic mail, send a postcard to these people – or wait until the holidays and send an early card with your new address highlighted.

- Change your signature on your e-mail messages to reflect your new address (and new phone number if applicable) and the date it takes effect.

- Order new address labels (or buy a rubber stamp) as soon as you know your new address.

- Keep all moving information in one pocket file folder or binder. Use a monthly calendar or day planner as a time-line for what to do and when.

- Make checklists for the old house that include items to buy/finish/fix and important phone numbers. Do the same for the new house.

- Make a floor plan of each room in your new home with big items (sofa, furniture, bookcases, etc.) shown in each room. Use this as a template as you decide what to take with you.

Packing (great opportunity to downsize):

- Don't pack stuff you don't use, clothing you don't feel good in, old décor, overabundance of linens and kitchen items, old hobbies, etc.

- Pack (or have movers pack) items that reflect who you and your family are today and where you want to be in the future. Your interests, tastes, and styles have probably changed over the years.

- As you pack, sort items into five areas: donate, return to/ give away to others, recycle, toss, and keep. Only pack the items you will keep and let go of the rest.

- Pack and label boxes by room and start by packing a room that doesn't get much use.

- Trust your judgment and resist the temptation to delay de-cisions. You'll save precious hours later.

- Use a thick permanent marker to mark each box with the name of the room. Mark what's in the box (in general) on two sides so you know the contents without opening the box.

- Combining two households? Weed out **before** you move. Compromise on what to keep from each household.

- Repack boxes you had in storage so they are 'move-worthy'.

- Be a green mover – get used boxes from local stores and your workplace. Recycle them when done.

Moving Day (be sure to get a good night's sleep):

- Have plenty of water and healthy snacks for the trip.

- Keep the following items in your car with you if you are traveling a distance: moving file folder; medications (family and pets); jewelry and other valuables; maps, GPS, directions; and a few toiletries (toilet paper, toothpaste, washcloth, and toothbrush).

- When you get to your destination, confine any pets to one room; place a 'Do Not Enter' sign on the door.

- Give children their own backpacks and include a favorite toy, snack, and book. Have clean pajamas packed so they are ready to sleep when the day is done. Have a night light in their packs for the first night in your new home.

- Pack a picnic dinner to eat on the floor if necessary.

Unpacking (pace yourself and enjoy the process):

- Make your bed first. Enough said.

- Take your time! The process is just as important as the end result so do it with care and have fun.

- Enlist family and friends to help. Don't be afraid to change your mind months later.

- Talk to your older children about how to setup their rooms to promote good organization with clothing, homework areas, and putting toys away.

- Post a list on the kitchen refrigerator of important phone numbers and a list of things you need to buy, fix, or remember to do.

- Hire a professional organizer. If time is of the essence or you want an objective eye to organize a new space, hiring a professional is money well spent.

When you are ready for company, have a housewarming party and invite the neighbors to promote good feng shui in your new home. Feng shui is when your home is set up to harmonize with the spiritual forces that inhabit it. Better yet, read Mary Lambert's book, *Clearing the Clutter for Good Feng Shui* (2001) and energize your home with feng shui enhancements. Also, don't forget to buy a big welcome mat for your new place!

SUCCESS IN ACTION

I worked with Toni for two moves. The first move was leaving the large home she shared with her husband to move to a small apartment. The second move was into a single home. Each time we worked together we talked about what her goals were, what her timeline was, what she was taking with her, and what she was leaving behind. Each move involved more purging. By the time she settled into her new house, she had only the things she really wanted and needed. She told me her home was finally a true reflection of herself.

5.4

Organizing and your significant other

"Holy Crap!"

Frank Barone, *Everybody Loves Raymond*

When it comes to organization in the home and how you feel about stuff, having a partner who thinks like you can make life easier. But it doesn't always work out that way. In my home, I am a thrower and my husband is a saver; therein lies most of our disagreements. I want to get rid of an item if we haven't used it in two years (because it's CRAP) – and he begs to differ. If you are both throwers, you both get rid of unnecessary items quickly and clutter is not an issue. On the other hand, if you are both savers, clutter is still not an issue because having clutter everywhere doesn't bother either of you. If you and your partner are opposites like my husband and I – the home dynamic can be dicey.

> It's important to start with common ground and figure out what each person must receive to be satisfied.

On the bright side, my husband has taught me how to respect other people's belongings. He told me why it's hard to organize and downsize his stuff and I've learned to understand his attachment to his belongings. Kathy Waddill, author of *The Organizing Sourcebook* (2001), knows that disagreements about organizing the home are often because partners disagree about what is important and what is CRAP. It's important to start with common ground and figure out what each person must receive to be satisfied. If one person has had enough of clutter and is ready to purge and the other one doesn't see what all the fuss is about, it can be painful.

As the owner of an organizing business, I find women are usually the chief organizer of the family, whether she works inside or outside the home. Unfortunately, if she doesn't like to organize, is too busy, or is a right-brain thinker (creative rather than analytical); she is still expected to be good at organizing because she's female. Many women struggle with Attention Deficit Disorder (ADD) and have trouble focusing on even the smallest tasks, let alone organize a home. Terry Matlen, author of the book *Survival Tips for Women with AD/HD* (2005), has great ideas for women who have gotten over the fact that they are not Martha Stewart and just need some help. Many of those women also call a professional organizer.

LET'S BREAK IT DOWN:

Here's what I've learned from my clients and my husband about organizing your home with your partner:

- First, get permission to organize your partner's stuff.

- When the offending clutter is in a common area, communicate why it bothers you (don't say because it's CRAP!).

- When organizing a space that doesn't belong to you, talk about the reasons why the area effects the rest of the family. Either way, work out a solution together.

- Hire a professional organizer to help you or your partner organize. In some cases, it's less stressful for the wife and the husband to have a third party work with them individually.

- If your husband is averse to having a professional organizer come into your home, point out the benefits to the whole family.

Have respect for your partner's belongings:

- You may view something as useless or unimportant, but it's not your decision to make. Keep the lines of communication open.

- Belongings can be very personal and tied to emotions. Making assumptions about the value of something shows little respect for the owner. Listen to your partner.

- The more respect you show for someone's belongings; the more willing the owner will be to let it go if and when the time comes.

- Never throw out anything without the owner's permission especially if it's a sentimental item. If he finds out, he'll never trust you to organize his stuff again.

When organizing a common area, ask for input from everyone who uses the space:

- Plan ahead and write everything down.

- Ask for suggestions on what works, what doesn't work, and vocalize your frustrations with the space.

- As you organize the space, get input on where the 'home' for items should be located.

- When the organization makeover is complete, bring everyone together to make sure everyone agrees on the location of items.

- Talk about how you can work together to keep it that way.

- Celebrate the finished product!

Finally, every client I work with (male or female) has different issues when it comes to clutter. The one thing they all have in common is that they want respect for their belongings and they want to be asked for their opinion about whether items stay or go. As your family grows and the dynamics of your family change, so do the ways your home is organized – be open to those transformations.

SUCCESS IN ACTION

Julia was starting to feel stifled by all the clutter in her home. She wanted to begin uncluttering because her stuff was no longer contributing to the life of her home and no longer a part of her plans for the future. Unfortunately, her husband of 25 years was not on the same page and her uncluttering made him uneasy and anxious. She began organizing and downsizing her own stuff so she could move on to the next stage of her life. Her husband started to see the benefits she was deriving from her efforts and slowly began to unclutter his own stuff. Julia takes hope from the steps (both big and small) she and her husband are making to unclutter their home and their lives.

5.5
Help children organize
for a calm household

*"Cleaning your house before your kids stop growing
is like shoveling your walk before it stops snowing."*

Phyllis Diller, *comedian*

When I was young and my mom sent my older sister and me to clean the room we shared, we had our own system: we threw everything into the middle of the floor, pretended we were the moms of very messy children, and complained the whole time while we put everything away. Pretty weird huh? We found a way to turn a chore into a game. As a parent, it can be a struggle to create a system to help children organize and deal with their stuff. We also have an obligation to provide limits for our children on what comes into the home and to set up a method for what goes out.

> We also have an obligation to provide limits for our children on what comes into the home and to set up a method for what goes out.

Peter Walsh, author of *It's All Too Much* (2007), says that "Kids are so over stimulated by the sheer volume of stuff in their home that they lose the ability to concentrate and focus." I helped my son let go of things he no longer wanted or needed by starting when he was very young. After each holiday and birthday, we went through his toys and decided what to give to 'boys who have no toys'. With new toys in view, it was easier to let go. When he got older we would go through his clothing together and he had friends who were thrilled to get his Penn State hand-me-downs.

Some parents hire me to help them organize their bedrooms first and then tackle the children's rooms – leading by example is their goal. On the other hand, some parents are surprised by all the stuff that their children have in their rooms. We talk a lot about how it got that way and where it's all coming from, e.g. birthday and holiday gifts from generous grandparents. Sometimes the truth is hard to face when parents come to the conclusion that they are being overly generous and indulgent. In some cases, their children want to have friends over and there's nowhere for these friends to sleep, sit, or play. Here are a few tips to assist children on how to set up their rooms and work toward a calm household – not a war zone.

LET'S BREAK IT DOWN:
Set the tone:

- Involve your children in organizing their room. Explain the benefits to them such as having friends over, a retreat from the rest of the house, and a space that's easier to keep clean.

- Ask your children what they like and what works well in their rooms – and what they don't like and doesn't work well.

- Integrate as many of their suggestions to increase the chance the arrangement will work. Ask them how they intend to keep clothing picked up, toys away, do homework, etc.

- Allow experimentation with the layout in the room even if you don't initially agree with it – allow children to think outside the box!

Children's room basics:

- Use a big trash can. Enough said.

- Use a big hamper. Don't expect them to leave their room to put dirty clothes in a hamper somewhere else (e.g. the bathroom).

- Go vertical when possible: hooks, shelving, book shelves, and shoe pockets on the back of doors. Clothing hangers can be difficult for young children.

- Leave floor space free for play and friends.

- Create zones in their rooms: sleeping, homework, reading, and playing.

Organization tools:

- Bins and baskets without lids are great. The less time spent on opening a lid or a drawer, the bigger the chance things will get put away.

- Use a clothes tree as the 'halfway' point for clothing: worn once but not yet ready for the washer – and it's up off the floor.

- Utilize toy boxes for big toys and bedding; otherwise they become a bottomless pit of rogue game pieces, doll body parts, and "I have no idea what that belongs to" stuff.

- Use furniture as room dividers instead of lining the walls with furniture – especially when two children share the same room.

- Employ bed risers to provide space under beds in smaller rooms.

Going forward:

- For children, less is more. Too much stimulation isn't a good thing. Agree on a system to let go of unneeded items: place a donation box in the hallway or somewhere close by. Mark the calendar to clean out after birthdays and holidays, etc.

- Boost children's self-esteem by listening to them when they want to make changes to their room. Unless they want to knock down a wall, most changes aren't permanent.

- Don't second-guess your children's decisions to let go of toys, childhood memories, or clothing – value their opinion.

- Ask (sometimes tell) grandparents to limit what they give your children or ask them for savings bonds or contributions to college funds.

- Give your children experiences and memories instead of stuff. My husband and I took our young nephew to a college football game for his 13th birthday and he started to talk about going to college for the first time. See Chapter 6.2 for more clutter-free gift giving ideas.

My greatest joy has been raising my son to be willing to donate or sell his clutter (a.k.a. CRAP). Giving him permission to let go of belongings he no longer wanted honored his opinion and his ability to make decisions. I'm so glad he's now a mature adult who grows attachments to people rather than stuff.

SUCCESS IN ACTION

Rosemary is a grandmother of two young children and wanted to display their artwork in the extra bedroom where they frequently stayed overnight. She already had some art she wanted to hang so instead of framing each piece (which would cost a lot) we put a binder clip on each side of the piece, strung fishing line on the back and hung them on nails throughout the room. As her grandchildren grow and bring more art to show grandma, they can easily switch out older art with new pieces.

CHAPTER 6

Go Green with your CRAP

Calvin treasured his book collection until his home became a branch of the community library.

6.1

Recycle to save the planet

"It's not easy being green."

Kermit the Frog

I've been a recycler since junior high school. We had an Ecology Bus (which was just a school bus painted to look like a jungle) parked at the school that collected newspapers and bottles. My mom and I would volunteer to work there – she was a recycler back when it wasn't fashionable. Even today, when I get a water bottle at a client's house or at an event, I'll hear her voice in my head to take it home to recycle it. To be honest, giving up my own water bottle habit still took a lot of effort.

> Bottled water produces up to 1.5 million tons of plastic waste per year.

If you are addicted to plastic bottled water like I was, go to Mother Nature Network website (www.MotherNatureNetwork.com) to find plenty of ways to break the habit. Did you know that bottled water produces up to 1.5 million tons of plastic waste per year[12]? Here are five compelling reasons from that website to stop drinking bottled water. Bottled water:

1. isn't a good value – in terms of profit, bottled water puts big oil to shame.

2. isn't any healthier than tap water.

3. means garbage.

4. means less attention to public systems.

5. means the corporatization of water.

You may be like some of my clients – they want to recycle, but their township doesn't recycle everything or not at all. It can take a lot of effort to set up a process to gather recyclables in a home, find a place that will take them, load the car, and deliver them – you have to be committed to being green. I'm a 'green' organizer which means I emphasize the environmentally-friendly principles of reduce, remix, reuse, and recycle. I enjoy helping clients set up a system to recycle just about anything and locating area recycling centers. Below is a general list of where to recycle certain items.

LET'S BREAK IT DOWN:
Electronics:

- Take non-working electronics to a designated place in your home until you have an accumulation (preferably in the garage or out-of-the-way place). Don't let them become clutter.

- When you are ready to recycle your electronics, go to www. BestBuy.com and find out what items Best Buy will recycle and if there is a fee. You can also go on the Internet and search for electronics recycling places in your area.

- Donate, sell, or give away old working models of electronics instead of keeping them around the house to collect dust.

Computers:

- Donate computers to schools or nonprofit agencies, but call first before you make the trip.

- Recycle any brand of non-working computers or accessories by dropping them off at any Goodwill Retail Store at no cost. They have a partnership with Dell called 'ReConnect' that safely recycles computers.

- Similar to televisions, Best Buy will also recycle computer screens. Find out if your local store charges a fee.

Personal papers, junk mail, newspapers, and magazines:

- Shred personal papers and keep your shredder where you sort your mail (see Chapter 4.1).

- Burn personal papers or junk mail if it's permitted in your area.

- Keep a box or bin close to where you sort your mail (inside a cabinet or underneath a table) to hold magazines, junk mail, and newspapers. Containers keep them in a neat pile until you are ready to put them out to recycle.

- Recycle junk mail with your local paper recycler along with newspapers and magazines if they'll take it. If they don't take junk mail, go to www.YellowPages.com (or *W&Y-White & Yellow Pages* smartphone app) and look for a recycling location near you. I take my junk mail to a local paper recycler about once a month.

Garage items:

- Collect hazardous waste containers in one area out of the way of children or pets.

- Take items to the hazardous waste collection sites in your area. Call the county or city to find out where and when. Our county recycles these items twice a year.

- Keep old tires up high on the rafters or walls of the garage until ready to be recycled. Our county recycles tires twice a year.

- Take items that could be used to build a house (e.g. light fixtures, old kitchen cabinets, old doors) to Habitat Restore locations (owned by Habitat for Humanity) and get a receipt for your taxes.

Miscellaneous:

- Cell Phones: crisis centers, homeless shelters, and electronics stores

- Ink-jet Cartridges: Office Max, Staples, Cartridge World (they refill my cartridges and some stores offer free delivery to businesses)

- Prescription Glasses: Lions Clubs International has donation boxes at local banks and stores (e.g. Walmart)

- Recyclable Materials: metal, corrugated cardboard, batteries, Styrofoam, appliances, glass, steel, plastics, and more – look in your phone book under recycling or go to www.YellowPages.com (or *W&Y-White & Yellow Pages* smartphone app) for recycling options in your area.

Here is a great website to find out how to recycle just about anything near where you live: www.earth911.org.

Reorganizing your home will make it easier to recycle and maintain new green habits. Use containers to set up a recycling center in the bottom of a closet, inside the garage, along a hallway or anywhere that is out of way but accessible to all. It's not easy being green, but isn't our planet worth it?

SUCCESS IN ACTION
My son moved to a new apartment in his junior year in college and the first time I visited I was pleasantly surprised by what

I saw. He and his roommates had set up a recycling center along the wall of the kitchen hallway. It included containers for every color of glass, plastic, newspaper, and cardboard. Luckily he lived in an environmentally conscious town and delivering these items wouldn't be too difficult. I'm glad one of my good habits rubbed off onto my son.

6.2

Clutter-free gift giving made easy

*"Anything that has real and lasting value
is always a gift from within."*

Franz Kafka, *German author*

Holidays and gift giving go hand in hand. However, shopping for the perfect gift gives some people a sense of dread – it's a lot of pressure. Many television channels add to the stress by counting down the shopping days until Christmas like it's a race to the finish. I really do love the holidays, but when my sister and I go shopping on Black Friday, it's hard not to be a scrooge. As a professional organizer, I work with clients who are having difficulty dealing with the clutter they already have and aren't looking forward to more stuff coming in the door. I also listen to clients who plead with grandparents to limit their gift giving to the kids, but are ignored.

> Clutter-free gifts are a gift of time, a memory, an experience, or a gift to help others who have needs beyond our imagination.

Annie Leonard, author of the YouTube video *The Story of Stuff*[13], points out the grim realities of our consumption not only at the holidays, but throughout the year. Do you know how much of what we buy is still in use six months after the date of sale in North America? 1%. That's right, 99% of the stuff we bring into our homes is trashed or unused by us within six months. The children in my extended family are blessed with generous relatives so I give savings bonds for birthdays and holidays. My gift may not be exciting to open, but they will thank me when it's time to pay for college, buy a car, or set up their first apartment.

If the thought of battling holiday crowds and spending money on a gift that will be forgotten before the snow melts gives you the blues, here's a list of clutter-free gifts to give to family and friends. Clutter-free gifts are a gift of time, a memory, an experience, or a gift to help others who have needs beyond our imagination. You can also practice clutter-free gift giving all year 'round! Let those you love know how much you care by going clutter-free this year. Let the retailers and advertisers know that the holidays aren't just about shopping for stuff. Here are a few of my favorite ideas for clutter-free gift giving:

LET'S BREAK IT DOWN:
Clutter-free gifts:

- Car wash coupons

- Cooking lessons

- Dance/yoga lessons

- Gym membership

- Movie tickets

- Museum membership

- Pottery/glass-making classes

- Savings Bonds (purchase online at www.treasurydirect. gov) and 529 plan contributions (think college)

- Self-defense classes (before females go off to college)

- Tattoo in honor of someone

- Tickets to the symphony
- Tickets to the theatre

Gift cards (not entirely clutter-free):

- Garden nurseries, home improvement stores, and bookstores
- Gas stations, grocery stores, and convenience stores
- iTunes, eMusic, and Ticketmaster
- Restaurants, coffee shops, and fast food restaurants
- Spa, facial, and massages

Nonprofit gift giving:

- Cash donation to a charity in honor of the recipient. Let the recipient know via a card.
- Give a gift certificate so the recipient can choose what charity to donate to at www.justgive.org.
- International Relief Fund gifts create lasting solutions to poverty, hunger, and injustice at www.oxfamamericaunwrapped.com.
- Green gifts for global impact at www.thegreenguide.com
- Life-sustaining gifts help abolish global poverty or renew our planet's environment at www.altgifts.org.
- Donate a farm animal in honor of someone at www.donate.worldvision.org or www.heifer.org.
- Find the closest toy drive at www.secretsanta.com.
- Give a tree in honor of someone at www.newgrowth.com.

- Donate a book on health information to communities all over the world at www.hesperian.org.

Gifts of time:

- For children: Go to lunch and a movie, on a day trip, to the museum, to a local college for a sports event, to the zoo, to a movie, on a picnic, to an amusement park, or to a playground.

- For a friend: Give local art studio classes, yoga lessons, book club membership, film club membership, scrapbooking classes, and pole-dancing classes (!).

- Babysitting coupons make great gifts for nieces, nephews, and grandchildren.

- Coupon book for your significant other: Make a list of the things you know your partner would enjoy and include practical and fun things: e.g., do the dishes for a week, make dinner for a week, do grocery shopping, foot massage for a week, stay home with the kids while you go out, flowers once a month for six months, a latte every Saturday morning for a month, etc.

Can't go clutter-free?

- Buy Christmas or Hanukkah cards that donate profits to your favorite charity.

- Buy gifts that support disease research (juvenile diabetes, breast cancer, etc.).

- Choose a gift that donates a portion of its profit to a non-profit agency. Verify the charity at www.give.org.

- Give a Ten Thousand Villages gift card (search for a store in your area).

- Purchase fair trade gifts at www.agreatergift.org.

- Support charities by purchasing t-shirts and gifts at www. CafePress.com.

- Support coffee farms in Uganda at www.ugandangold. com.

Finally, there are plenty of things to do instead of shopping at the holidays. Drive around neighborhoods at night in pajamas (take hot chocolate and popcorn) and look at the light displays. Visit the gardens and nurseries that decorate for the holidays and don't miss the local holiday concerts at churches, schools, and colleges. I know I'll be watching the movie *It's a Wonderful Life* (1946) for the 1,000th time with my own popcorn and hot chocolate. Enjoy!

SUCCESS IN ACTION

Chris decided to move to a new home to be closer to her grandchildren. She talked to me about her role in their lives and that her grandchildren would be coming to her home after school and on weekends when their parents were away. As we talked about setting up his and her rooms in her new home, she commented on how much stuff her grandchildren got for the holidays. As a result, she decided that savings bonds were the perfect holiday gifts to give to her grandchildren. The relief that crossed her face when she made that decision was noticeable. She realized that one-on-one time with Grandma was the gift, not more stuff.

6.3

Too many books? Share the wealth!

"The world is a paradox: too many people have too much of everything and too many people have too little of anything."

Barry Schwartz, *Psychologist and author*

I was not a reader as a young child, nor did I read for pleasure as an adult because I always had a 'required' reading list for undergraduate and graduate school. Reading for fun was foreign to me. Fast forward to today: I finally discovered reading for pleasure. For me, reading is a delight, an escape, and a way to slow down at night before I go to sleep. Using reading a book as my carrot, I organize my work and stay more focused if there's a good book to look forward to at the end!

> There are so many children and adults who could use your unneeded books.

When I need a new book, I often borrow from friends, family, or clients. Otherwise, I take a trip to the community library. Even though booksellers are going out of business across the nation, I hope community libraries will always be around. I'm still amazed I can pick out a pile of books and walk out the door without paying for them. Of course, I do have to return them, but that's a bonus – they don't clutter my home. Call me cheap, but I like going green by reading books already in print and not creating a demand for more trees to be chopped down.

If you bought this book as an eBook, you saved a tree! The Kindle, iPad, Nook, and other eReaders are the ultimate in green. I have begun to download free books on my iPhone so I'm catching the bug. I hope these devices will encourage more child readers and persuade more people to give up some of their printed books to be shared with others who have no books. There are so many children and adults who could use your unneeded books. If you have children, how many books do they have and how many of those books are your children still reading?

Here are some statistics that might surprise you about children, books, and literacy from the literacy resources on Heart of America Foundation's website at www.heartofamerica.org:

- The home environment - specifically the availability of reading material - is a stronger predictor of later academic achievement than socioeconomic status[14].

- Sixty-one percent of low-income families have no books at all in their homes for their children[15].

- On average, children in economically depressed communities have 0-2 age appropriate books in their homes[16].

- Children in middle-income communities have an average of 54 books in their homes[17].

- Children in high-income communities have an average of 199 books in their homes[18].

Below I have listed suggestions for donating, selling, and buying books. Be aware that many places no longer take encyclopedias, National Geographic magazines, textbooks, and old library books. If no one wants your books or magazines or they are moldy/musty, pages missing, or ragged, it's okay to recycle.

LET'S BREAK IT DOWN:

- New and used bookstores: Sell or trade your books at these stores. If you must buy, buy used and save a tree (www. Amazon.com is a great website for used books). Look for book consignments in your phone book or on www. YellowPages.com (or *W&Y-White & Yellow Pages* smartphone app).

- Public and community libraries: Call them or go on their website to find out what they will take before you drop off books. Some accept duplicates to sell at book fairs. Find local libraries in your phone book or on www.YellowPages. com (or *W&Y-White & Yellow Pages* smartphone app) or go to Friends of the Library at www.folusa.org.

- Thrift stores: Many thrift stores accept books so they can sell them and use the proceeds to assist underserved families.

- Books for Soldiers: Go to www.booksforsoldiers.com where soldiers make requests via an online forum and you can send literary care packages directly to them.

- International Book Project: Go to www.intlbookproject.org and find out how this nonprofit humanitarian group has been sending books to orphanages, schools, and churches worldwide for over 40 years.

- Prison libraries: Go to www.writeaprisoner.com/books-behind-bars to see regularly updated requests from prison libraries. Needs range from law dictionaries to Spanish-language novels, so be sure to consult individual listings.

- Local schools and hospitals: Make a list of your local schools and hospitals – call them or go on their websites to find out if they have any need for books.

- Additional websites for textbook and book donations:
    - www.bringmeabook.org
    - www.iamfoundation.org
    - www.betterworldbooks.com
    - www.booksforafrica.org

If you give your books to nonprofit agencies, you may be able to take a tax deduction for your donation (consult your tax accountant). When your personal library gets too full and you are ready to share the wealth of knowledge and entertainment your books could provide, there are individuals just waiting to enjoy your literary treasures. It does take some effort, but the only thing better than a good book is sharing a good book!

SUCCESS IN ACTION

I have assisted a number of clients with organizing their home libraries. The first question I ask a client is "What will you look under to find the book you want?" I have helped organize libraries alphabetically by title, by author, by genre, by type of religion, by fiction/non-fiction, etc. I also ask clients to look out for books they will never read again so we can donate the excess. Sometimes they donate one box and sometimes I leave with my car loaded. Either way, the client ends up with an organized library that is all their own. For smartphone users, see the app *My Library* to record your entire personal media collection.

6.4

When enough is enough

"He who knows that enough is enough will always have enough."

Lao Tzu, *founder of Taoism*

When I work with clients who have had enough of their clutter, we unearth many things that the client isn't using, but could be useful to someone else. For example, these are some of the random things I find in client's homes: used bath towels, unfinished sewing projects, lamps that don't work, unused antique furniture, clothing that needs tailoring, old wedding dresses, broken antique furniture, unframed art pieces, favorite childhood clothing, old tangled gold jewelry, random old coins, and watches. Items like this lay around long enough to become a nuisance (a.k.a. CRAP) and many people just trash them.

> Did you know that Americans throw away an average of 4.6 pounds of trash per person per day?

Did you know that Americans throw away an average of 4.6 pounds of trash per person per day? Australians are next on the list and they only throw away 2.7 pounds of trash per person per day. In her book, *The Story of Stuff* (2010), Annie Leonard provides these and other eye-opening statistics on the waste that we perpetrate every day when we trash our stuff. I wonder how much of that trash is useable or still 'good' and the owners just didn't know where to take their stuff. In my experience, people are willing to donate their items; they just don't know how or where their items might be useful.

Professional organizers can come to the rescue of many people who are struggling with letting go of these items or finding someone to repair or refurbish items. Organizers are generally well connected in the community and serve as a resource to provide names of handymen/women, cleaning services, repair shops, tailors, carpenters, jewelers, electricians, and a number of other businesses. A list of those businesses and services is one of the most helpful tools I have available to my clients, family, and friends.

Below is a list of suggestions for where to donate or sell different items. I've also added some of my favorite places to have things fixed, repaired, or given new life.

LET'S BREAK IT DOWN:

Donate it:
Animal shelters can use:

- dog cages

- leashes and collars

- leftover dog and cat food and cat litter

- old towels, blankets, and newspapers for animal bedding

- pet taxis for small animals

Freecycle.com (search by city):

- Post free local online ads to unload what you don't need at no charge to the receiver.

- Receive what you need for free by going to the website and searching for your item (I get free packaging materials to use for eBay from this site.).

Goodwill Retail Store, Hope Rescue Mission, Salvation Army, local churches or synagogues welcome receipt of:

- clothing and accessories
- furniture, small and large appliances
- kitchen items, collectibles, home furnishings, and décor

Habitat ReStore for Habitat for Humanity:

- Donate anything to build or furnish a home: doors, windows, light fixtures, furniture, etc.
- Arrange for free pick-up from some stores.

Libraries in your community:

- Donate books, audio books, and DVDs.

Women's shelters, career centers, and homeless shelters (check websites for 'wish lists') usually request items such as:

- blankets and sheets
- children's books
- clothing for office work
- toiletries and make-up

Sell it:
Auction houses:

- Arrange to have an on-site tag sale at your home.
- Unload a large quantity of items at one time (especially furniture).

- Receive cash upon pick-up or wait until sold.

Bookstores with used books:

- Sell or receive store credit for books, audio books, and DVDs.

Consignment and resale shops:

- Shop owners will choose what clothing and accessories they will sell.

- Get cash or store credit for your items.

- Some stores accept children's clothing, toys, and equipment.

CraigsList.com:

- Post free local ads online: cash only.

eBay.com:

- Locate a trading assistant to sell your items on eBay.

- Take a class and sell items yourself. Find a local trainer from eBay University by going to www.eBay.com and click on customer support.

Local newspapers:

- Classified ads still work.

Reputable jewelers:

- Sell old gold, sterling silver, and platinum jewelry.

- Sell coins and watches.

- Some jewelers give credit to purchase new items.

Fix/Repair/Refurbish it:

Carpenters:

- Refinish antique furniture.

- Remake or repurpose antiques (I had the shelves of a low buffet strengthened to hold liquor bottles.).

- Have chairs recaned by the Blind Association in your area.

Frame shops:

- Frame art, certificates, or child's art.

- Frame cross-stitched pieces from children's pillows, vintage quilts, etc.

Tailors:

- Tailor or alter clothing.

- Create throw pillows from a childhood dress, wedding dress, or sweater.

- Mend clothing that isn't ready for the trash.

Upholsterers:

- Recover antique stools and chairs.

- Make throw pillows from antique fabric or have cushions made for window seats and old church pews.

Finally, when you donate items to nonprofit agencies, consider these tax credit basics:

- If you itemize your deductions, you may be eligible to deduct your donations. Consult a tax accountant or <u>www.irs.gov</u> for details.

- You must estimate the fair market value of the items donated. Use *IRS Publication 526-Charitable Contributions*[19] *and IRS Publication 561-Determining the Value of Donated Property*[20] for further information. If you use TurboTax, the fair market value is computed for you.

- You must file IRS form 8283-Noncash Charitable Contributions[21] with your 1040 if you donated over $500 or above of total fair market value.

- Go to the Salvation Army website at <u>www.salvationarmy-usa.com</u>[22] or the Goodwill Industries, Inc. website at <u>www.goodwill.org</u>[23] for valuation guides for donated clothing and goods.

Disclaimer: This information is not meant to replace your tax accountant or information available from <u>www.irs.gov</u>.

When enough is enough, donate to your favorite charity, sell stuff to get cold hard cash for what you really want and need, or repurpose something old and make it new. It does take some effort, but you'll feel good about leaving your stuff out of the landfills.

SUCCESS IN ACTION

Ruth and Robert were selling their large family home after 25 years to move into a smaller home closer to their grandchildren.

To stay focused on selling their home, they approached their downsizing like a full-time job. They prepared a list of the projects they needed to tackle in order to clean out the entire house. They called me to assist them with the list they prepared. Each day we tackled the projects on their list one by one. They didn't take time for long lunches and evenings out with friends until the job was done and their house was ready to sell. In a few short months their house was sold.

6.5

Are you suffering from Affluenza?

"How will the value of your days be measured?
What will matter is not what you bought, but what you built;
not what you got, but what you gave."

Michael Josephson, *ethicist and author*

Do you feel constant discontent with yourself and what you own? Are you encouraged to buy without limits by advertisers? Are you suffering from 'stuff' overload? You may be suffering from the social disease 'affluenza'. This is the unhappy condition of overload, debt, anxiety, and waste resulting from the dogged pursuit of more. *Affluenza* (2005) is an innovative film that outlines the impact that buying so much stuff is having on our families, communities, and the environment. I highly recommend this film which is available from Bullfrog Films at www.bullfrogfilms.com. The producers use personal stories and expert commentary to show how consumerism, commercialism, and rampant materialism have given us more stuff while our quality of life deteriorates.

Affluenza is the unhappy condition of overload, debt, anxiety, and waste resulting from the dogged pursuit of more.

I showed this film each time I taught a class on organization at a local community college. I believe that before we learn about organizing our stuff, we also need to understand where it's all coming from, why we are bringing it in the front door, and the ultimate effect it is having on our quality of life. *Affluenza* has appealed to audiences from freshmen orientation programs to marketing classes, and from consumer credit counselors to religious congregations. After watching it, you'll understand how our lives have been taken hostage by our stuff (a.k.a. CRAP) and you'll never shop the same again.

In the film, Dr. Richard Swenson, best-selling author and award-winning educator, points out that our society was happiest in 1957, which was reported in an article by Myers and Diener (1995) entitled *"Who is Happy?"* Then the age of possession overload started. We went from a nation that prized thriftiness, simple living, and high ideals to the ultimate consumer society. Swenson says, "Never before has so much meant so little to so many!" Americans throw away seven million cars per year. Our rate of consuming far exceeds the ability of the planet to absorb our pollution. Is it any wonder that one of the definitions of consume means exhaust, pillage, and destroy?

Finally, there's an organization called the Campaign for a Commercial-Free Childhood (CCFC), which is a coalition of professionals and parents who raise awareness about how corporate marketing undermines children's wellbeing and advocates limitations on the impact of commercial culture on children. In reality, this commercialization is the link between many of the most serious problems facing children and our society today such as childhood obesity, youth violence, and rampant materialism. CCFC works for the rights of children to grow up – and the freedom for parents to raise them – without being undermined by commercial interests. Find them on the web at www.commercialfreechildhood.org.

If you think you may be suffering from affluenza, please read on:

- Just as children need limits in order to grow into responsible adults, our homes need limits on the amount of stuff we bring into them. If your stuff is spilling out of the closet, off the dresser, off the desk, off the bookcase, off the counters, out of drawers, on the floor, and out of cabinets, you are probably suffering from CRAP overload or affluenza.

- If you have trouble locating things because there is too much other stuff in the way, begin to downsize your belongings. Simplify your life so you can find what you really want and need in your home.

- Always have a donation box available on each floor of your home so when you bring something in, you can donate something else.

- If you find yourself saying, "I don't want my children to live like this", then it's time to start uncluttering. Think about how materialism may be affecting your children.

- If your house suffers from CHAOS, Can't Have Anyone Over Syndrome (see www.FlyLady.net), then it's time for a change!

The film *Affluenza* ends with a prescription to cure the disease: families are working and shopping less, spending more time with friends and family, volunteering in their communities, and enjoying their lives more. These people are opting out of the consumer chase and choosing voluntary simplicity instead. How will your days be measured? Could you benefit from a little more simplicity and a little less affluenza?

SUCCESS IN ACTION (OR NOT SO MUCH IN THIS CASE)
Gwen was in her 80's and was overwhelmed by her four-story home full of stuff. She had tried to enlist her husband and her

children to assist her with downsizing, but didn't have much success. Her family wanted to rent dumpsters and throw the contents of the house away when she and her husband passed away, but this gave Gwen nightmares.

She decided to attend one of my organizing classes at the local community college, but realized that downsizing 50 years of belongings would be a mammoth task. Even though Gwen was encouraged to take my class, her family was unwilling to hire my services to assist them with the process (money was not an issue). She called me in tears to express her frustration and I gave her additional information to supplement the classroom materials in hopes that her family would step up and help her begin the process.

CHAPTER 7

Special Categories of CRAP

ollin was getting a lot of business done on his long flight, but his fellow travelers didn't appreciate it.

7.1

Simplifying the holidays

*"I will honor Christmas in my heart
and try to keep it all the year."*

Ebenezer Scrooge, *rehabilitated crabby old guy*

Thanksgiving is my favorite holiday. I have wonderful childhood memories of visiting my aunt's family in Maryland, where we would spend the weekend eating, putting puzzles together, and laughing a lot. Fast forward to the present, we spend Thanksgiving at my sister's house with about 25 family and extended family present – it's crazy, but a good crazy. The day after Thanksgiving our family tradition is to go to breakfast with my parents (they treat) and my sister and I fuel up for our traditional 'Black Friday' shopping. Yes, even though I'm not a fan of all the excess CRAP that the holidays bring, we like to take the opportunity to spend the day together, eat nice meals, shop at an unhurried pace, and enjoy the holiday decorations.

> Take the word 'should' out of holiday planning.

When some of my clients talk about the holidays, I hear the words 'dread' or 'depressed'. They don't look forward to the influx of more stuff when they are already struggling with a mountain of things they don't know what to do with. Simplifying the holidays is critical for these people because they need to feel some sense of control over what happens in their homes even though the world around them is in over-the-top holiday mode. In their book, *Organize Yourself!* (2005), Eisenberg and Kelly have a whole chapter dedicated just to party planning, which very few organizing books have. The bottom line for holidays and for parties is making sure **you** enjoy yourself *(no, really)*.

Simplify your holidays by deciding at what level you will celebrate and take the word 'should' out of holiday planning. "I should have all the relatives over for dinner", "I should bake 10 dozen cookies", "I should handwrite 200 holiday cards", or "I should put up a sequoia in the family room" is not the way to start your holiday season. Just because mom did it one way, doesn't mean you have to do it that way. Start your own traditions and stick to it no matter what others are doing or want you to do.

LET'S BREAK IT DOWN:
Schedule for less stress:

• Plan ahead and schedule the big activities well in advance on the calendar: e.g. wrapping gifts, sending cards, baking, decorating the house, etc.

• Plan to shop when the stores aren't so busy – many stores are open late at night.

• Avoid the crowds (and the stress) and shop online. Look for free shipping deals.

Try clutter-free gift giving (See Chapter 6.2 for ideas):

• Give the gift of time: an experience, an outing, dinner and a movie, baby-sitting, etc.

• Give a gift that is consumable (candle), plantable (a tree), edible (cookies), or a gift card to a favorite restaurant.

- Listen and abide by friends and family wishes when they request no gifts. Go to dinner or a movie together instead.

Traditions aren't set in stone:

- Some traditions are important and some are less important; discern the difference so you don't feel guilty especially if your life or your finances have changed.

- Consider starting new traditions especially if you have new family members.

- Traditions are meant to invoke good feelings, not dread or guilt. My husband and I have a tradition to start the holiday season by celebrating Advent dinner with our neighbors.

Create a budget and stick to it:

- Don't allow advertisers or retailers decide how you should celebrate the holidays. Know your limits.

- Make a gift list before you buy so you don't overbuy or overspend. There are no 'shoulds' when it comes to gift giving.

- Visit that 'gift closet' that you designated to hold previously bought gifts before you shop for more gifts. Do you have items that could be regifted?

- Take stock of your food supplies and staples before you bake or cook and make use of what you already have in the pantry.

Cards are a gift, not an obligation:

- Send holiday cards if you want to or send a New Year's greeting instead when you have more time.

- Enter your addresses in the computer and print out labels for a real timesaver. Have young family members help to affix stamps and return address labels.

- Use the Internet to send real greeting cards using www. SendOutCards.com/vali. You can use your own handwriting and signature and it saves money and time!

Plan holiday parties well in advance:

- Decide who, when, what, and how. This helps you focus and stay on track.

- Keep a calendar of what to do when to stay on schedule.

- Freeze food ahead of time; elicit the help of family and friends.

- Go through your supplies first and then shop for what you need.

Make room for impromptu holiday fun:

- Take time to drive around to the see the neighborhood decorations or ask the neighbors over for drinks or hot chocolate.

- Look for local holiday concerts and shows (some are free of charge).

- Participate in holiday activities that serve others: volunteering at the food bank, wrapping gifts for charity, serving meals at shelters and churches, or donating to Toys for Tots.

Entertaining overnight guests:

- Set up the guest room like a nice hotel: fresh sheets and pillow cases, bath towel, washcloth, fresh seasonal flowers, glass for water, and a mint for the pillow.

- Ask your guests what they want for breakfast. Don't prepare a feast if they just want a bagel and a cup of tea.

- Let your guests know what your plans are for each day so they can arrange their day. Guests generally want to spend time with their hosts, but they would also like to come and go as they please.

Organize for the holidays before they begin and you'll have a recipe for success. Take the word 'should' out of your vocabulary and celebrate the holidays on your own terms. The goodwill you create will last throughout the coming year!

SUCCESS IN ACTION

Holly was overwhelmed by her Christmas decorations because she had accumulated a mountain of stuff over the years. It included gifts from the children in her classroom (she was a teacher), gifts from others, heirlooms, and a lot of CRAP she didn't want. Because the thought of putting it all out at Christmas gave her angst, she was tempted to not put it out at all. I suggested that she schedule a date well in advance of the holiday to begin uncluttering those decorations. She will look at each item and decide what should stay and be displayed, what could be offered to her grown children, and what should be donated. As a result, holiday decorating for the future would be a pleasure, not a burden.

7.2

Organizing for baby 101

"Your children need your presence more than your presents."

Jesse Jackson, *civil rights activist and Baptist minister*

Getting organized before my son was born was not only essential, it was a lifesaver. Having a baby was the most wonderful and most stressful time of my life. I remember getting ready to leave the hospital and I honestly couldn't believe they were allowing me to take my son home with me because I didn't have a clue what I was doing. Not being a 'baby person' or having babysat when I was young left me feeling totally out of my element.

> I honestly couldn't believe they were allowing me to take my baby home with me.

I did however give in to all my nesting instincts before my son was born: cleaning, disinfecting, and baby-proofing. Thank goodness I had an older sister to help me decide what I needed for my son's room because I didn't buy anything unless I received it at a baby shower. I read the book, *What to Expect When You're Expecting* (2008) by Heidi Murkoff and Sharon Mazel and it was my 'baby bible'. If you don't feel you have the baby gene (*like me*), I highly recommend this book. I'm also looking forward to seeing the movie that's coming out in May 2012 by the same name!

Finally, I met with a few pediatricians before I decided who would best fit my personality. I needed someone knowledgeable, but not someone who would make me feel even more inept than I already did. I also wanted someone who had the same philosophy as I did when it came to breast feeding and circumcision. Then I filled out all the preliminary paperwork at the doctor's office so the first visit with the baby in tow wouldn't take so long.

Even when you are organized, new babies will cause a huge change in your current system – be flexible. If you aren't organized, use this occasion to help prioritize the stuff in your home. Be willing to rework your system as they grow and welcome advice from family and friends on what systems worked for them.

LET'S BREAK IT DOWN:
Before baby:

• Smartphone users can download the app *My Pregnancy Today* by BabyCenter. Enter your due date and you can get answers to questions as you go through your pregnancy (*I would have loved this during my pregnancy over 20 years ago!*).

• Have a plan for who is taking you to the hospital and who is taking care of other siblings when you are ready to deliver.

• Pack your hospital bag and leave it by the door or in the car. Don't forget comfy pajamas, favorite bedtime items (lavender-scented eye cover), and clothing to wear home.

• Get a tote organizer to carry baby stuff. Make sure it has a long strap to carry hands-free.

• Wash (in Dreft) and sort baby clothes by size; have some larger sizes (clothing and diapers) just in case your baby grows fast.

- Have medical cards and paperwork ready to go. Find out what your insurance covers and let them know when you are due including the name of your pediatrician.

- Cook and freeze a few ready-to-eat meals (or ask someone else to do this).

- Have bottles and feeding items readily accessible in the kitchen. Reorganize a few cabinets to get ready for the influx of bottles, baby food, and formula.

Room set-up:

- Resist buying too many outfits for your baby. Your baby won't end up wearing everything you have (trust me) and the number of choices can overwhelm you.

- Setup a changing table/area on each floor of your home.

- Stock up on diapers, wipes, butt cream, spit cloths, and Onesies (*I cried when my son grew out of these*) for each changing area.

- Designate a baby room with other siblings in mind and arrange the room so everything is within reach, especially when you're changing diapers and holding on to a wiggling baby at the same time.

- Baby-proof low cabinets and drawers with baby-proof locks. Cover sharp corners of fireplaces and coffee tables with padding.

- Place crib on an inside wall to avoid the cold in winter. Use room darkening shades.

After baby:

- Smartphone users can download the app *My Baby Today* by BabyCenter. It has a calendar, checklists, and photo albums.

- Babies cry. Enough said.

- Try to relax and enjoy your baby while he or she is small; babies grow fast.

- Take time for yourself. Take 15 minutes to soak in a warm bath, read a book, or take a cat nap. This is a must.

- Try to have someone with you the first week you are home for an extra hand.

- Sleep when your baby sleeps and shower as soon as you can manage each day (it makes you feel better).

- Keep doctors, friends, and relatives' phone numbers in your cell phone. Post numbers on the refrigerator for helpers.

- Relax your neatness standards for the rest of the house while babies are small; being overrun with diapers, bottles, and baby toys will not last forever.

- Curb your buying for your new baby. Less is more and babies need your time, not more stuff.

Finally, just because you are now a mom doesn't mean you magically know everything about babies. Never be afraid to ask for help and try not to feel guilty if you have doubts about your new role. If all else fails, talk to a nurse or a professional counselor (*it worked for me*). If you take it a day at a time, you'll learn to enjoy this wonderful albeit stressful time!

SUCCESS IN ACTION

Debbie called me when her son was three months old. She and her husband were overwhelmed with baby stuff and couldn't seem to fit it in to their current household system. We started in her kitchen by taking everything out of her cabinets. We incorporated baby bottles, formula, food, dishes, etc. into the cabinets. She decided what she would no longer need in her kitchen and put those items on a shelf at the bottom of the basement stairs. She also donated a lot of items that she knew she'd never use again. The result was a more realistic set-up for current baby items and room to grow in the years ahead.

7.3

Photographs everywhere – Now what?

"Today more of us in America than anywhere else in the world have the luxury of choice between simplicity and complication of life. And for the most part, we, who could choose simplicity, choose complication."

Anne Morrow Lindbergh, *aviator pioneer*

My mom has a bottom drawer in her antique secretary that is stuffed with random photos dating back to her wedding in 1956. I'm tempted to pull them all out and categorize them, but I wouldn't want to take that pleasure away from her (*yeah, right*). It can be overwhelming to try and organize your old photographs and with all the beautiful scrapbooking that's going on – it's intimidating to know where to start. I tell my clients not to make it more complicated than it has to be. For me, the simpler the better – my scrapbooks wouldn't win any awards, but they do the job.

> My scrapbooks wouldn't win any awards, but they do the job.

Photographs are some of the most precious belongings we have. In her book *Let Go of Clutter* (2001), Harriet Schechter points out that although survivors of catastrophes regret losing photographs the most, the overabundance of unorganized photos is also a source of stress. That flood of pictures "usually end up languishing in envelopes, baggies, baskets, and/or boxes, just waiting for that proverbial rainy day." I saved my scrapbooking/photo album making for snow days, because it was not my favorite task. When the snow day arrived, I would tackle the project for the whole day.

Digital photography has given us an opportunity to share old pictures with family and friends in beautiful new ways at weddings, graduations, anniversary parties, and funerals. Many businesses can take your old photographs and scan them for you so you can show them digitally or print them. My favorite photos are all on my iPhone and a lot of people simply share pictures on Facebook or Twitter. We are saving lots of trees by not printing and it's easier to share our photographs with a larger audience without getting out the glue and the photo corners. Unfortunately, I also see the over-the-top side of scrapbooking where people buy to excess – and seldom get around to making the albums. Scrapbooking can be a great example of choosing complication over simplicity.

Here are a few tips on how to organize photographs, work with digital photography, or just get started.

LET'S BREAK IT DOWN:
Sorting a backlog:

- Gather all the photographs in your home and take them to one location.

- Set up a table, a comfortable seat, and good lighting. If possible, pick a location that you can keep set up until you are done.

- Schedule a time once a week to sort the photos until you catch up.

Organizing:

- Divide photographs into categories that make sense for you. No method is wrong – organize by date (the easiest and most common method), by family member, vacation, or event.

- Invite a family member or friend to help you sort, purge, and organize.

- Allow time for pouring over your pictures, reminiscing about people, and talking about events. Make it fun, not just a chore.

- Work on putting photos into albums (digital or physical) once a month to keep current – choose snow days while enjoying the warmth or hot summer days while enjoying the cool.

Storage for physical photographs:

- Wait to buy containers/albums until you are done sorting so you know what type you need and how many.

- Choose the type of container: accordion files, photo boxes with tabbed dividers, scrapbooks, or photo albums by how you will store your photographs. If you use shelving, buy albums or boxes of the same size.

- Choose a cool, dry, and dark area for storage of photographs and albums.

- Use 'acid-free' and/or 'archival' storage boxes or albums.

- Consider storing negatives in a separate location or scan photographs (this is ideal) on your computer and throw out negatives.

Working with Photographs:

- Throw away or delete poor quality photographs.

- Send similar or duplicate pictures to friends and family. You don't have to make it beautiful, just send them.

- Print photos or save online when you finish a roll or when the memory card is full so you don't get behind.

- Choose brand name paper if you print your own photographs so they don't fade away (*I learned this the hard way*).

- Write the date on physical photos so you don't lose track (don't count on your memory).

- Use your own software or online software such as www.Shutterfly.com and www.Snapfish.com to organize your digital photographs.

- Date digital photos and organize into folders on your computer by events, dates, or people so they are easy to retrieve and share with family and friends.

- Have a back-up system on your computer so you don't lose precious memories.

Additional options:

- My sister-in-law sends a Christmas eCard as a calendar of photographs to our whole family and I love it. I forward it to friends to share.

- Collect photographs for your children and give them in a gift box when they get older. They can either create their own scrapbook or scan them into their computer. This takes the pressure off you and allows them to choose the method of display.

- Enlist the experts to digitize your old and tattered photos: e.g. MotoPhoto stores, Creative Memories consultants, www.SaveMyPix.com, www.CelebrateYourPhotos.com, or www.HeritageMakers.com. Then decide how to store and display them.

If you've got a backlog of pictures, remember that it took years to accumulate them. Be patient with yourself as you organize your photos and remember the process is part of the enjoyment. How you start or how you decide to organize your photographs is totally up to you – no one way is best. Try not to make it more complicated than necessary and then enjoy the walk down memory lane.

SUCCESS IN ACTION

When Robin hired me, she had a backlog of photographs that was driving her crazy. She wanted a place to spread them out so she could work on them whenever she wanted. First, we uncluttered a corner in her finished basement and added a big fold out table, comfortable chair, and good lighting. I worked with her to gather all the photographs from every corner of her home and put them in the selected area. We set up a system to start organizing her photos by date. Now she can work on her photographs when she has the time and doesn't have to clear a space to work when she's inspired.

7.4
Traveling – Getting away from stuff

"There must be more to life than having everything."

Maurice Sendak, *American illustrator and writer*

I love to travel, especially when I can travel light and someone else is doing the driving. Thanks to my husband who is willing to stay home with our two dogs, I can travel to visit our son, go on trips to write this book, and tag along with my friends when they travel for work. Recently, I took a bus to New York City and spent three days with my son who was living in Manhattan. I took only a backpack with enough necessities for two nights. It was a pleasure and a luxury to travel unencumbered.

> The purpose of taking a vacation is to have fun, relax, and refresh so we can continue living our lives.

Traveling light is fun but it's also risky. What if you forget something? Will you be able to do without it? For some of my clients, preparing to travel is a nightmare. Getting ready to go on vacation is stressful enough just trying to get everything done. But when homes are unorganized, it's hard to assess what the basics are let alone pack them to go away on a trip. Jennifer Ford Berry, author of *Organize Now!* (2008), suggests that we take time to plan before we leave on vacation and continue the slower pace after we return. After all, the purpose of taking a vacation is to have fun, relax, and refresh so we can continue living our lives. One of my colleagues used to brag that she hadn't taken a vacation in years. What's up with that?

I also look forward to traveling because wherever I go, life is simpler and I can pay attention to what's really going on instead of what I have to get done. Vacations are also about enjoying ourselves without taking care of our stuff. Also, when I travel for business or go on a working vacation, I get some of my best work done because I am away from daily chores, interruptions from the telephone, e-mail, and snail mail. Whether you are traveling for pleasure or business, be sure to plan ahead to get the most from your time away.

LET'S BREAK IT DOWN:

- Organize your road trip. Don't forget the GPS, MapQuest (print out or use from your smartphone), or a paper map.

- Use the smartphone app *Around Me* to locate banks, hotels, restaurants, or pharmacies wherever you travel.

- Get E-ZPass (electronic toll collection system). This is a no brainer for anyone who travels.

- Use written checklists. Don't risk forgetting something important.

- Be flexible. All the planning in the world doesn't mean mishaps won't occur. Don't sweat the small stuff – leave time for spontaneity.

- Choose electronic tickets. There's nothing better than bypassing a long check-in line at a busy airport or train station.

- Travel light. Check the airline's website, but two carry-ons are allowed on most flights (that includes your handbag). Besides the money you save by not checking a bag, you minimize your choices and your decisions during your trip.

- Limit your clothing. Select items you can mix and match. Wear one set of jewelry that matches all of your outfits (*yes, it is possible*).

- Buy trip cancellation or interruption insurance. Give yourself peace of mind.

- Downsize your handbag. Just carry the essentials: limit cash, irreplaceable jewelry, or keys.

- Pre-pack toiletries. Choose a clear one-quart bag and pack small liquid items (3 oz. or less) instead of repacking each time you travel.

- Pack comfort snack foods (especially for children).

Here's my list of business travel to-do's (especially on a plane, train, or bus when you're not driving):

- Do a 'brain dump'. This is when you write down everything that's on your cluttered mind. Then decide what to do about it, when to do it, if you really need to do it, or if you can't do anything about it (and can therefore forget about it).

- Take your 'reading pile'. Carry your accumulated unread magazines and miscellaneous mail and throw it away as you read each item. Rip pages out of magazines, journals, etc. that you want to keep or make notes for future reference.

- Organize your cell phone. Delete unwanted items and add missing contacts. Clean out pictures, missed calls, inboxes, and outbox.

- Purge your computer files. Reorganize documents into folders, and delete unnecessary items. Put old files into folders on other drives to avoid cluttering current projects.

- Clean out your purse/wallet/briefcase.

- Schedule fun stuff. Place entries on your calendar for family time, vacations, and personal projects to ensure you'll take the time to do it.

There is more to life than having everything, it's called vacation. If the thought of traveling or going on vacation makes you sweat, plan ahead and decide to travel light. Getting away for a week, a day, or even an afternoon can help keep busy lives in perspective and provide time to focus on what is most important. Wherever my son ends up living in this world, I hope to travel light and visit him as often as he'll allow!

SUCCESS IN ACTION

Sheila did a lot of traveling for her job. She felt overwhelmed each time a trip was looming and she wanted to change that. First we packed a toiletries bag with smaller versions of the items she used every day and she used the supplies only for travel. In that same bag, we included a list of items she only had one of so she didn't forget to pack them: e.g. medications, cell phone charger, make-up, etc. Finally, we packed a separate briefcase (that would hold her laptop) with office items to be used only for travel: e.g. highlighter, paper clips, Post-it notes, extra mouse, and AA batteries. Going forward, she felt ready to travel at a moment's notice.

7.5
Organizing for college –
Young and old(er)

*"Organizing is what you do before you do something,
so that when you do it, it's not all mixed up."*

A. A. Milne, *English humorist and author*

My first career was working in a college financial aid office for almost 20 years. When my son was approaching college age, I was excited about this new stage in his life and was glad for the experience I gained as an employee of a college. My job gave me a perspective unlike any other and it also came in handy when my friends were sending their children off to college or a trade and technical school. When I attended college in the late 1970's as an undergraduate, the percentage of high school graduates who enrolled in two- or four-year colleges was 49%. When my son went to college 35 years later, the percentage went up to a whopping 70%[24].

> Even though I worked hard to be organized – it was a challenge to keep my head above water.

I also went back to college for my Master's degree as an adult so I had additional insight into what it was like to be an adult going back to college. The Association for Nontraditional Students in Higher Education (ANTSHE) reports that students who are over 25 make up 47 percent of the new and returning student population on many of today's college campuses. Unlike the traditional age student, most adult students are juggling responsibilities between a job, a family, and their studies. Even though I worked hard to be organized – it was a challenge to keep my head above water.

Whether you or your child goes off to study at a technical school, a traditional four-year college, or a community college, the process can be fraught with decisions – so being organized is a big part of success. When you're organized, you can focus on your studies and get the most out of your education. Here are a few suggestions from my experience to help you or your child organize before, during, and after this life-changing transition called college.

LET'S BREAK IT DOWN:

Before college:

- Attend college nights at your local high school. Ask lots of questions. There are no dumb questions – just the ones not asked.

- Apply for college admission within deadlines. Applying early is critical if your child wants acceptance into a certain major, on-campus housing, or early acceptance for college funding. Admission deadlines for adults can vary with the type of program. Consult the school.

- Apply for financial aid within deadlines. File the Free Application for Federal Student Aid (FAFSA) to apply for all types of grants, loans, jobs, and scholarships from federal, state, and college sources. File online at www.FAFSA.com. Contact the college for any additional required applications for financial aid.

- Meet with the staff in the Financial Aid Office. If you have special circumstances in your family: divorce, layoff, death, two in college at the same time, etc., meeting face-to-face with aid professionals is ideal.

- Meet with the head of the academic department. Young adults can ask questions about faculty, graduate rates, and placements rates. Older adults can inquire about transferring credits, life experience credits, and online classes.

During college:

- Keep important phone numbers for the college on your phone: e.g. Health Center, Residence Hall Office, Dean of the department, Registrar, Financial Aid Office, and Business Office.

- Seek help from tutoring centers. That's what your tuition is paying for.

- Continue to file financial aid forms within deadlines.

- Meet with your academic adviser. Make sure you are on track to graduate within your timeline.

- Parents:

  - Be advised that college departments may or may not be able to discuss your child's information with you. Privacy acts may not allow it. Ask for the college's Family Educational Rights and Privacy Act (FERPA) policy.

  - Be prepared to let your child make his or her own decisions and mistakes. It's better to make mistakes in the college environment than in the real world.

  - Restrain yourself from becoming a helicopter parent (constantly hovering). Colleges will treat your child as an adult – you must too.

  - Keep in touch with your son or daughter through social media. Text or communicate on Facebook or Twitter.

Calling every day may be too invasive for some teenagers who are on their own for the first time, but by all means, keep the lines of communication open.

After college:

- Prepare your resume. Visit the Career Development Office at the college and seek online help from www.Monster.com, www.Job.com, www.LiveCareer.com, and www.ResumeBuilder.com.

- Get business cards printed with your degree, skills, and contact information. It's easier to network and job hunt with a business card.

- Establish an account on LinkedIn to build your professional network at www.LinkedIn.com.

- Change your voice mail message. Greetings should reflect a professional tone – "Wassup!" isn't an appropriate greeting for prospective employers.

- Keep your options open. The type of position or type of employer can vary from business to business.

- If you are already employed, send a letter to your Human Resources Department to notify them of your advanced degree.

Finally, as a parent don't let anything go unsaid in order to keep your child safe and healthy (*I didn't*). After that, your children must make decisions based upon their judgment (*scary, I know*). If you are the one attending college, organizing first will make the process more enjoyable and you'll be able to focus on studying and test taking. Above all, take it a day at a time and have fun!

SUCCESS IN ACTION

Henry hired me to help with paper organization for his two college-age children. He was overwhelmed by all the paperwork he was receiving from the college and the banks for his children's student loans and the parent educational loans he borrowed on behalf of his children. First, we sorted all the paperwork in three piles, child #1, child #2, and parent. Then we looked at each piece of paper and eliminated duplicates, unnecessary papers, and filed the rest. Finally, we designated a separate file folder for each child. Each folder had a sheet taped on the outside of the folder with important phone numbers for the college, student ID#, lender phone numbers, the child's social security number, and any other critical information. Henry was finally ready to tackle the mail that was yet to come!

CHAPTER 8

Thinking Outside the Box about CRAP

Tam's collector plates were her most valued possession until she tried to use them to pay her college tuition.

8.1

The Story of Stuff – a.k.a. CRAP

"Capitalism, as it currently functions, is just not sustainable."

Annie Leonard, *author of The Story of Stuff*

Boy, I'm glad Annie Leonard said it and not me. She is the author of *The Story of Stuff:* a 20-minute YouTube video[25] that I wrote about in Chapter 6.2. In the video, she explains the process of manufacturing consumer goods and how we are trashing the planet with our stuff. I'm not anti-capitalist, but as a professional organizer, I am at the end of the distribution cycle when stuff is obsolete, broken, forgotten, or just plain never used. Leonard defines stuff as manufactured or mass-produced goods, including packaging, electronics, clothes, shoes, cars, toasters, etc. She says "It's the stuff we buy, maintain, lose, break, replace, stress about, and with which we confuse our personal self-worth." In other words, what she calls stuff, I call CRAP.

With just 5% of the world's population, the United States is consuming 30% of the world's resources.

The New York Times calls *The Story of Stuff* a "sleeper hit in classrooms across the nation." The video is simple but thought-provoking. I don't believe you will shop or think the same way about stuff after viewing it. I used this video in an organizing class I taught at the local community college. To understand how to organize, the class first needed to understand what we are doing to the planet when we buy all this stuff that we want to organize. Organizing is not just about finding a place for everything and everything in its place. It's about making room for the things we really want and need in our lives.

Annie Leonard's video (and the book of the same name) takes us through the process of consumer goods production: extraction, production, distribution, consumption, and disposal. Much of our trash is a result of **planned obsolescence** which is when manufacturers design a product to break or become useless so we toss it and buy a new one. It's not our imagination when our appliances don't last nearly as long as our parent's appliances lasted. The other part of our trash is a result of **perceived obsolescence** which is where we get rid of stuff that is perfectly useful because advertisers have convinced us that we need the latest technology, fashion, model, or upgrade to be trendy. After all, we have to keep buying to contribute to the health of the economy don't we? Very few people are immune to this kind of pressure (*including me*).

So what is the result of all this trash? Our rate of consuming far exceeds the ability of our planet to absorb our pollution. Leonard points out that with just 5% of the world's population, the United States is consuming 30% of the world's resources. If everyone consumed at that rate, we would need three to five more planets!

Speaking of a finite planet, have you seen the animated Disney movie *WALL-E* (2008)? WALL-E is the name of a trash compactor robot who lives on earth by himself with only a little roach as his sidekick. He's alone because the earth could no longer sustain plant life to grow food, and it became so full of stuff and trash that everyone had to move out into space. As important as Disney felt this theme of excess was, they **still** produced a plethora of *WALL-E* collectibles. What a powerful message they could have sent if they had decided NOT to flood the earth with *WALL-E* paraphernalia. Even the DVD comes in four formats each with its own list price and a slightly varied mix of extras. Can you say 'overkill'?

After you've watched *WALL-E* with your children, you may want to bribe them to watch *The Story of Stuff* on YouTube. The similarities between the two are incredible: they teach our kids a lot about reducing, reusing, and recycling albeit in very different ways. Annie Leonard and the staff at The Story of Stuff Project have created great resources for you, your kids, and their teachers about these issues. It is available at <u>www.thestoryofstuff.org</u>.

- *The Story of Stuff* book is available on the above website. It's the expanded version of the video with much more about how our obsession with stuff is trashing the planet, our communities, and our health.

- For high school teachers and students, The Story of Stuff Project collaborated with Facing the Future, a nonprofit organization that offers sustainability and global issues curriculum. Together they created *Buy, Use, Toss: A Closer Look at the Things We Buy*. This free two-week curriculum is available at <u>www.facingthefuture.org</u> and includes 10 fully-planned lessons aligned with national science and social studies standards.

- For the younger set, Annie Leonard worked with the television stations WGBH-Boston and PBS Kids to develop "Loop Scoops", a series of fun two-minute videos that get kids thinking about the stuff in their lives. Things like: What is this made of? Where did it come from? Who made it? And what happens when I throw it away? Go to <u>www.pbskids.org/loopscoops</u> to check out the videos. Share them with young people and pass them along to teachers for use in the classroom.

- For the life-long learners among us, Annie Leonard recently released a Reading Guide for *The Story of Stuff*, which is available on <u>www.thestoryofstuff.org</u>. This free guide includes discussion questions, ideas for enhancing or starting your book club, and a Question & Answer section with Annie Leonard. Grab a copy of *The Story of Stuff* from your library – or from a local bookseller – and then download the Guide from their website.

- You can view, download, and share all of *The Story of Stuff* project movies available on their website, which includes the *Story of Bottled Water, Story of Cosmetics, Story of Electronics* and the newest movie, *Story of Broke.*

- For more information about how to green your school, check out the people at the Green Schools Initiative. They are a nonprofit started by parent-environmentalists who have mobilized to improve the environmental health and ecological sustainability of American schools. Go to www. greenschools.net.

In her book, *The Story of Stuff*, Annie Leonard presents a vision for change and hope for a brighter future. By reading her book, you'll learn how to be a part of the solution. Her message is far from anti-Capitalism; it's anti-trash the planet. Be a part of the change!

CRAP CHALLENGE

- Download and watch *The Story of Stuff* on YouTube. Make a list of five things you'll do to reduce the trash you send to the landfills.

- Watch the movie *WALL-E* with your children. Have them make a list of three things they will do to stop trashing the planet.

- Walk through your home and identify ten things you can donate to a local charity.

8.2

Rethinking consumption

*"Like so many Americans she was trying to construct a life
that made sense from things she found in gift shops."*

Kurt Vonnegut, *author of Slaughterhouse Five*

As a professional organizer fascinated with consumerism, I am intrigued by how my clients think about their belongings before and after an uncluttering session. Before uncluttering, many clients talk about shopping without a list, buying something twice because they can't find the first one they bought (*no, you aren't the only one*), or buying before they knew whether an item would fit, work, or be useful. After uncluttering, I teach them to take a list when they go shopping, take stock of what they have before they buy, and understand that everything they bring through the front door has strings attached and has to be taken care of in some way.

> Advertising is one of the reasons we've been programmed to shop until we drop, or max out our credit cards, whichever comes first.

Baseball used to be America's favorite pastime, but I think we can all agree that these days it's probably shopping. Many of us shop for the sake of shopping without much thought at all, which is my definition for 'unconscious consumption'. One of the best places to practice unconscious consumption is the mall, and the biggest mall is in Minnesota called the Mall of America[26]. It is 4.2 million sq. ft. with over 500 stores, 50 restaurants, 14 movie screens, museums, a wedding chapel, an amusement park, and an aquarium. It attracts 40 million visitors each year – more than Disneyland – and there are more than 50 hotels within 10 minutes of the mall. There even used to be a Barbie fountain with Barbie shoes floating in it (*gag*).

Another example of a colossal mall is Core Pacific City, also known as the Living Mall[27]. It is a shopping center in Taipei, Taiwan with a total floor space of 2.2 million sq. ft. The complex consists of 12 above-ground stories and 7 underground levels. As one of the first of several large-scale malls in Taiwan, the planners of the Living Mall hope to change local consumer behavior to Western-style one-stop shopping (*I am not sure if that's a good thing or a bad thing*).

My favorite illustration of unconscious consumption is the television shopping networks. I affectionately call them 'home invaders' because, while we have control of our remotes, shopping channel emcees can hold us captive 24/7. They use what I call the 'Stepford Wives' technique of sales: use perfect-looking people to sell must-have items in an over-the-top manner to convince us to buy things we don't need, don't have money for, and never knew we wanted until we tuned in (*whew!*). QVC television viewers and Internet shoppers alone spent more than $7.37 billion in the year ending January 2010[28]. This spending may help keep the economy going, but that's a staggering amount to spend just on stuff. That spending is why many of my clients call me – they are overwhelmed by their stuff and they've had enough.

Advertising is one of the reasons we've been programmed to shop until we drop, or max out our credit cards, whichever comes first. Companies used to produce goods to fulfill needs. Now they manufacture needs to produce goods. To sell those goods, advertisers play on our emotional vulnerability by:

- Over-using words like 'designer', 'collectible', 'gourmet', 'retired', 'official', and 'discontinued' to get us to buy almost anything (*remember Beanie Babies?*).

- Trying to convince you that you'll be an outcast or worse if you don't buy their product. My favorite radio commercial example of this was: "Don't spend your holiday weekend sitting on inferior furniture!"

- Producing false needs to persuade us to buy items outside our value system and beyond our means, e.g. buying a larger house or a more expensive car than we really need or can afford.

- Using words like: 'only 20 left', 'avoid disappointment and future regret', 'limited quantity', or 'only one minute left' to encourage a quick sale.

- Promoting 'one day sales' as exceptional – until they hold another one next week.

- Telling us to call in the next 10 minutes and they will 'double the offer', but 'only for a limited time' – or until the next time the commercial airs.

Here are a few ways to rethink our buying habits instead of continuing to clutter our homes with unnecessary CRAP.

- Use our own values to determine what to buy instead of letting advertisers dictate our purchases.

- Be informed consumers – spot those over-used advertising words to see what's really on sale.

- Take control of what comes in our front doors and tell 'home invaders' we aren't for sale. See Chapter 1.4 for ideas.

- Write down your 'dream list'. This is a list of large ticket items you want to buy in the future, e.g. a new home, new car, vacation, college tuition, etc. Look at this list when you are tempted to buy something that isn't on the list.

- Buy **used** instead of **new**. Look for words like 'consignment' and 'gently-worn'. Buying a certified used car is a bargain compared to buying a brand new one.

- Shop local instead of long distance. Supporting unique and interesting local businesses, big and small, helps the local economy and lowers our carbon footprint – this is loosely defined as the total set of greenhouse gases caused by the life of an individual.

- Try eco-shopping. These are products that are low-impact and environmentally-friendly. Go to www.Shopgreen. pricegrabber.com to find more than 20,000 products, ranging from organic lip gloss to EnergyStar appliances. This site donates 5% of profits to environmental charities.

Just think of the collective difference we could make if we became just a little more mindful of how we spend our hard-earned money. Practice a little less 'unconscious consumption' and little more conscious consumerism. I'm up to the challenge, are you?

CRAP CHALLENGE

- Make a dream list and put it in your purse or smartphone. My dream list included a new kitchen and it helped me curb my spending until my kitchen was a reality.

- Shop with a purpose, not for entertainment. If you feel the need to spend money, buy something that someone else needs and give it to them (*works for me when I get the retail therapy itch*).

- Make a list of five locally owned retail stores and coffee shops. Post them on your refrigerator and remember to patronize these businesses when you need a gift or gift card.

8.3
Organize to be idle

"Some of us need to discover that we will not begin to live more fully until we have the courage to do and see and taste and experience much less than usual."

Thomas Merton, *monk and Roman Catholic writer*

I love the spring: planting my garden, planning summer vacation, going to graduation parties, and, most importantly, sitting on my screened-in porch to read a good book. Organizing my home and my life allows me to have the time to enjoy all these fun things – including being idle. One of my favorite books is *How to Be Idle* (2005) by British writer Tom Hodgkinson. This gem of a book is a charming, tongue-in-cheek, 'loafer's manifesto' on how to be idle. It questions the basic assumptions of running from event to event and why our stuff is sucking up so much of our time.

> We shouldn't clutter our homes with stuff that brings no lasting commitment beyond the initial thrill of the purchase.

In Hodgkinson's chapter entitled 'The Idle Home' he refers to the business of "living to the simplicities". He says that it is essential for an idler not to commit that "terrible bourgeois sin" of trying too hard and that your ideal should not be an ordeal. He explains how home design magazines prey on our insecurities so that we buy the décor pictured in the magazines to get the look of the celebrities homes. We shouldn't clutter our homes with stuff that brings no lasting commitment beyond the initial thrill of the purchase. His mantra is that to be truly idle you have to be organized and efficient. With less stuff, there is less to keep track of because any mess ends up stealing time from you. You can see why I love this guy!

In his chapter on holidays, Hodgkinson quotes a realist writer George Gissing who wrote, "Our notion of a holiday is to rush in crowds to some sweltering place with our miserable children being lugged about." What an awful scene, but isn't there some truth to that? Gissing also wrote that "work in itself is not an end; only a means; but we nowadays make it an end, and three-fourths of the world cannot understand anything else." Believe it or not, Gissing wrote all that in 1892! The more things change, the more they stay the same! If we could be happier with less stuff we could work less because we would need less money – and have more time for being idle.

Finally, Hodgkinson points out that the word 'leisure' comes from the Latin word 'licere', which means 'to be permitted'. We must actually permit ourselves to have leisure time. Many of us give the responsibility of scheduling our free time to others and have only ourselves to blame. Don't let others tell you how to vacation, how to spend your free time, or when to enjoy your life. Organize your life and your home so you can live simply and have idle time, on your own terms, to recharge your batteries.

In 2005, I vacationed in Ajijic, Mexico with a good friend. When I go away on vacation, I go to get away from the mental and physical stuff of my life so I can take a break and just 'be'. During that trip, it was never more apparent to me that to be happy, I didn't need a lot of stuff. I didn't go to a resort, but to a small town where people live simply, eat simply, and seem very content. I spent ten days enjoying local food, local sites, and lots of idleness. I realized that part of the reason I was able to sit around and do a lot of nothing, is that my 'stuff' didn't follow me – I had nothing to take care of. Here's my short list on how to be idle when you aren't on vacation.

LET'S BREAK IT DOWN:

1. Unclutter, unclutter, unclutter. The less stuff you have, the less time you need to spend taking care of it.

2. Listen when people talk to you. It takes a lot of will power and idleness to calm your mind and be present.

3. Turn off your phone or at least the sound (*I know, it's shocking, but phones have an on/off button*). I'm not suggesting hours at a time. Just ten minutes at a time can be freeing.

4. Turn off the television or music and listen to nothing for one evening. Calm your mind. It takes courage to just 'be'.

5. Just drive for one whole week, e.g. stop talking (or texting) on the phone, putting on make-up, eating, changing clothes, or writing while you are driving. I use *Voice Memos* on my iPhone to avoid writing while I'm driving.

6. Eat at a restaurant by yourself. Take a book if you wish, but learning to sit without talking is the key.

7. Take yoga. If only for one hour a week your mind is idle, it's worth it.

8. Sleep in at least once a month. Being idle in a comfortable bed is a luxury.

Learning how to be idle isn't easy. Many years ago, I was a 'Type A' personality: constantly running, saying 'yes' to everyone, and doing 150% of everything I took on. As a result, my health suffered and I was forced to drastically adjust my life. I changed my job (thanks to my boss), starting taking yoga, and began reading books for pleasure. I am now a 'B+' personality and proud of it. I had to learn how to be idle and it changed my life for the better. You can too.

CRAP CHALLENGE

- Choose two items from the list above and do it. Let me know how it goes.

- Tell me how you organize in order to be idle.

- Take note of how many 'things' you can do without on your next vacation. Try to duplicate that feeling at home.

8.4

Embrace your space

"Stuff has power, and the stuff we own has power – power for good or power for ill."

Peter Walsh, *author, television celebrity, and professional organizer*

One of my favorite experiences as a professional organizer was taping a radio program called 'Organize This!' which used to air on the Internet. The format of the program consisted of my ruminations (*and rantings*) about CRAP. CRAP of course is my acronym for Clutter that Robs Anyone of Pleasure. Don't get me wrong: I love my stuff, but I enjoy it and honor it by using it or displaying it – otherwise, it's gone.

> When we are pushed to make choices, it doesn't take long to realize that it's not the stuff in your life that is important, but the people who make it richer.

During the radio program I offered organizing tips and explored the root of disorganization. I was happy to receive lots of positive feedback by e-mail. The biggest surprise was how far and wide my listeners were. They listened in Alaska, Arizona, California, Florida, Hawaii, Texas, and Washington. There were also international listeners with organizing issues in Australia, Brazil, Canada, Germany, India, and Kuwait.

Their comments mirrored the same issues my clients bring to me every day such as being overwhelmed by stuff, living with a pack rat, or selling and downsizing a home.

In some cases, the e-mails from these listeners went deeper and revolved around life transitions due to personal crisis in their family, their life, and their country. One listener from India said his country was so unorganized it was hard for the people to be organized in their businesses and in their homes. He suggested that a professional organizer could make a lot of money in India, but it's hard for me to comprehend what it would be like trying to help people organize in countries that have larger social and governmental issues than we do in the United States.

I also wonder how homeowners in other countries view their clutter. What does too much stuff in Japan look like compared to too much stuff in the United States? For instance, the average American home grew from 983 square feet in 1950 to 2,349 square feet in 2006 according to National Association of Home Builders statistics[29]. That's a 140 percent increase! Of course, averages vary greatly from rural to urban settings, but the average size of a Japanese home is 1,021 square feet according to a 2003 Housing and Land Survey conducted by the Japanese Ministry of Internal Affairs and Communications[30]. The average home in India is even less. Can you imagine fitting all your stuff into a space that small?

When my son attended Culinary School in Manhattan, he lived in an apartment that was 200 square feet. Surprisingly he had sufficient room for all the necessities and a little more – including a full size bed. His room didn't include a bathroom or shower, which were both down the hall. He broke the room into two zones and he repurposed a large dresser to hold kitchen and personal items in addition to his clothing. He now shares a bigger flat in Brooklyn with four other roommates and has reorganized his belongings to fit that space. He has learned to truly embrace his space wherever he lives.

If you go to an IKEA home furnishings store, visit the sample living spaces on display. One of them is 590 sq. ft. and it's amazing. IkeaMalaysia posts a video series featuring their interior designers giving tips on how to squeeze every last inch out of a living space[31]. They boast being able to organize a 430 sq. ft. apartment; a 118 sq. ft. combo bedroom/living room; and a remarkable 29 sq. ft. bathroom with room for laundry facilities. Their advice: when you can't go outwards, go upwards and find objects that can do double-duty.

A few years ago, one of my clients was moving to China. She had to prioritize her stuff in order to pack for the move. As a seasoned, cross-continent mover she knew she would have to shed one-third of her belongings, store one-third, and take one-third with her. Imagine if you had to quickly prioritize your belongings and shed two-thirds of your possessions. What is most dear to you and what is just 'stuff'? How much can you do without? What is non-negotiable because it is precious and necessary? Stuff has power for good or ill. When we are pushed to make choices, it doesn't take long to realize that it's not the stuff in your life that is important, but the people who make it richer.

I often work with clients who struggle to embrace a space. They aren't happy in their homes for a variety of reasons:

- "Our house is too small."

- "We are living in my in-law's old house and we are finding it hard to make it our own."

- "I liked the house I lived in before better."

- "I'm not sure how long we'll be in this house."

- "We were supposed to build a new house and that fell through."

When homeowners don't embrace their space, they aren't happy when they come home. They constantly feel like a visitor in their own home. When I work with clients to help them reorganize their home to live within its parameters I ask them what they don't like about each room and how we might transform the room to make it work for them. 'Making do' only works for so long. Life is too short to be waiting for the next house (see Chapter 1.3).

While I watched the news of the devastation caused by the earthquake and tsunami in Japan in April 2011, and the tornado in Joplin, Missouri in May of 2011, my heart broke for the families who lost their homes. One news reporter said even though the families survived, they still had to come to grips with the fact that everything was gone. Even though my farm house has been a money pit, I appreciate it more and more – it has been a labor of love and if it were gone tomorrow, I would miss it. Regardless of your circumstances, what country you live in, and how big your space is, embrace your space. Only fill it with the things that remind you of people and places that you love. Anything else is just CRAP.

CRAP CHALLENGE

- Make a list of five things you love about your home.

- Make a list of five things you don't love about your home and would like to see changed.

- Put together a list of short-range and long-range goals to make changes in your home and attach a timeline for completion.

8.5
Die clutter-free

"There's a name for people who have the most stuff.
They're called hoarders.
Back in the day, they were just called grandmothers."

Ellen DeGeneres, *comedian*

In their book *Die Broke: A Radical Four-part Financial Plan* (1997), Stephen M. Pollen and Mark Levine, explain their revolutionary philosophy of dying broke by asking these questions:

* "What good will money do for you when you're dead?"

* "Why can't you take care of your family while you're alive?"

* "Isn't it foolish for your family to have to wait for your death to benefit from your wealth?"

I agree with the authors, but for reasons that have to do with clutter, not wealth. Here are my questions:

* "What good will your stuff do for you when you're dead?"

* "Why can't you share your stuff with your family while you're alive?"

* "Isn't it foolish for your family to have to wait for your death to help you downsize your belongings?"

So I'm taking poetic license and concluding this book by introducing a radical new concept: Die clutter-free. Stay with me, I'm just brainstorming. In my organized, utopian, fantasy world, there would be a law (*okay, suggestion*) that between the ages of 65-75, people must start to downsize their possessions. It could be called the "The Great DUMP" (Downsize Useful stuff to Maintain our Planet). People would begin to unclutter long before they are ready to actually leave their current homes. Items that are no longer being used, are no longer needed, or are just taking up space in the home could be passed down to family, recycled, donated to people who need it, or sold to get money for things the homeowners really need.

> "The Great DUMP" (Downsize Useful stuff to Maintain our Planet).

Professional organizers could lead The Great DUMP effort to assist these early downsizers. Retail thrift stores for Goodwill, Salvation Army, Habitat for Humanity, and Hope Rescue Mission would get federal dollars to open additional stores to handle the intake of many more items from the public. Additional large warehouse stores (let's call them DUMPing Grounds) would be established to accept everything from clothing to furniture items on consignment. You designate a certain charity to receive the profits from the sale of your items. It would be chic, politically correct, and cool to shop at these stores. These stores would charge less sales tax. You must bring along your own shopping bag or box to shop there. Private entrepreneurs could open their own facilities, but they wouldn't get as much of a tax break. Finally, large brick and mortar eBay stores would be established to sell items to local clients and sell items on www.eBay.com to the world market.

If you start downsizing your stuff at age 65, you get the highest tax incentive. The amount of that incentive goes down as you age – so it's prudent to donate as early as possible. Before you feel compelled to send an e-mail to ask me if I've calculated the cost to the U.S. Government for all of this, the answer is no. I figured I would leave that up to the private entrepreneurs who will see this as a win-win proposition.

In an article written by Barbara Flanagan (1991), Patrick Hare, a Washington, D.C. urban planner, coined the phrase 'Peter Pan housing' to describe housing for people who think they'll never grow old. "Their Never-Never Land is the nation's endless spread of suburbs and exurbs where real-life laws and codes only reinforce the illusion that America is eternally, expansively young." Jon Pyoons, PhD, a professor at UC Davis School of Gerontology[32] explains this housing as having "narrow hallways, slippery bathrooms, and houses crammed full of stuff." If you saw the pain in the eyes of many of my clients who realize they are physically unable to move one piece of furniture let alone unload a whole house, you would understand why our country would benefit from this early downsizing concept. These clients are just realizing the truth behind the words, "You can't take it with you".

As a professional organizer, I have worked with a wide range of clients who need to downsize their homes. I work with the homeowner before it is time to leave the house. I also work with the children or power of attorney to clean out the home after the homeowner has passed away or gone to live in an assisted living facility. The biggest difference between these before and after clients is the amount of trash thrown out. For clients who begin the process early, we productively spend our time donating items to an average of five different charities and I sell some items on eBay to get cash for the client.

For clients who have stayed in their homes long after they are able to care for themselves or their homes, we throw out many more items. In a few of these instances, the neighbors were helping the clients stay in their homes by running errands and doing household chores. During that period however, the homeowners' immobility prevents them from taking care of their pets and their home including the second floor, the attic, and the basement. As a result, items that are stored in hot attics, wet basements, plastic wrapping, or out in the open air are usually ruined. These items decay, rust, melt, break, deteriorate, or get feasted on by mice – and they are no longer useful to anyone. Filling a dumpster with items that could have been salvaged with a little prior planning is very sad.

Finally, think about the belongings in your home. If everything you didn't touch, use, appreciate, or even look at for a period of two years just disappeared, how much would be gone, and how much would you miss it? That amount would vary from room to room of course, but if you can't see it, you aren't enjoying it, you don't need it, and you aren't using it, why do you have it? There are so many people who need our used items. Isn't there a better way? If there is, let's figure it out fast – our children and our planet are counting on us.

CRAP CHALLENGE

- Make a list of the charitable organizations in your area that will receive items when you are ready to downsize and unclutter. See Chapters 6.1 and 6.4 for ideas.

- Ask your children now if they want the things you've been saving for them in your attic or basement.

- Make a list of five precious items you want to hand down to your family. Write down the stories about those items so others understand why these things mean so much to you.

EPILOGUE

I look forward to sharing more practical tips, green ideas, and ruminations about CRAP in my next book!

Please send suggestions, ideas, and comments for:

- future chapter subjects
- clutter-free gifts (Chapter 6.2)
- additional myths for not unloading CRAP (Chapter 1.5)
- how you organize to be idle (Chapter 8.3)
- websites with organizational tips that really work
- smartphone apps that help you stay organized

Send your organization success stories for the **Success in Action** sections and maybe you'll see yourself in my next book.

Thanks again for buying my book!

Vali G. Heist

Contact me!
Vali G. Heist, M.Ed.
Certified Professional Organizer®
www.thecluttercrew.com
Like me on Facebook
Follow me on Twitter: @ValiOrganize
Leave feedback on Amazon.com

REFERENCES

(Smartphone apps, website addresses, and web references were updated when this book was published.)

SMARTPHONE APPS

Around Me by Attorno A Me S.R.L.-find out information about your surroundings

DonationApp-a Blue Book for your used stuff

iDonatedIt by BMG Certified Public Accountants-tracks non-cash charitable deductions

Key Ring Reward Cards by Mobestream Media Inc.-scan and save all of your loyalty cards in your smartphone

Meal Planning by Food on the Table-meal planning and saving money at the grocery store

MealBuilder Pro by Wombat Apps LLC-healthy meal planner and grocery list

Mint.com Personal Finance by Mint.com-manage and pay bills

My Baby Today by BabyCenter-resource for every new parent

My Library by Josh Pressnell-personal media collection organizer

My Pregnancy Today by BabyCenter-resource for any parent-to-be

OfficeDrop by Pixily, Inc.-scan, search, organize, and store paper files

Pageonce-Money & Bills by Pageonce, Inc.-manage and pay bills

Spider Solitaire, Microsoft Corporation-Vali's favorite time waster

Voice Memos on iPhone-record ideas while driving to write down later

White & Yellow Pages by Avantar LLC-search for individuals and businesses

BOOKS AND PUBLICATIONS

Berry, Jennifer Ford. *Organize Now! A week-by-week guide to simplify your space and your life.* Ohio: North Light Books, 2008

Crouch, Chris. *Being Productive: Learning how to get more done with less effort.* Tennessee: Dawson Publishing, 2009

deGraaf, John and Boe, Vivia. *Affluenza.* Pennsylvania: Bullfrog Films, DVD, 1997, 2005

Dellaquila, Vickie. *Don't Toss My Memories in the Trash.* Mountain Publishing, 2007

Disney/Pixar. *WALL-E.* DVD, 2008

Dudley, David, *Conquering Clutter*. AARP Magazine, January and February 2007

Egan, Marsha. *Inbox Detox and the Habit of E-Mail Excellence.* 2008

Egan, Marsha. *Inbox Detox and the Habit of E-Mail Excellence.* eBook, 2011

Eisenberg, Ronni and Kelly, Kate. *Organize Yourself!* New Jersey: John Wiley & Sons, Inc., 2005

Flanagan, Barbara. *A New Kind of Old Folks' Home.* San Francisco Chronicle, April 21, 1991

Gross, Kim Johnson. *What to Wear for the Rest of your Life*. New York: Springboard Press, 2010

Hemphill, Barbara and Wig, Jennifer. *Taming the Paper Tiger in the Digital Age @ Home*. eBook, 2011

Hodgkinson, Tom. *How to be Idle: A loafer's manifesto*. New York: HarperCollins Publishers, 2005

Izsak, Barry. *Organize Your Garage in No Time*. Canada: Que Publishing, 2005

Jay, Francine. *Frugillionaire: 500 Fabulous Ways to Live Richly and Save a Fortune*. New Jersey: Anja Press, 2009

Kapra, Frank. *It's a Wonderful Life!* DVD, 1946

Kolberg, Judith and Nadeau, Kathleen. *ADD-Friendly Ways to Organize Your Life*. New York: Brunner-Routledge, 2002

Kuper, Donna Smallin. *Declutter Your Home and Make Money Now!* eBook, 2012

Lambert, Mary. *Clearing the Clutter for Good Feng Shui*. New York: Friedman/Fairfax, 2001

Lehmkuhl, Dorothy and Lamping, Dolores. *Organizing for the Creative Person*. New York: Three Rivers Press, 1993

Leonard, Annie. *The Story of Stuff*. New York: Free Press, 2010

Lillard, Debbie. *Absolutely Organize Your Family: Simple solutions to control clutter, schedules and spaces*. Ohio: North Light Books, 2010

Lillard, Debbie. *Absolutely Organized: A Mom's Guide to a No-Stress Schedule and Clutter-Free Home*. Ohio: North Light Books, 2008

Matlen, Terry. *Survival Tips for Women with AD/HD: Beyond Piles, Palms & Post-its*. Florida: Specialty Press, Inc., 2005

Morgenstern, Julie. *Organizing from the Inside Out*. New York: Henry Holt and Company, LLC, 1998

Murkoff, Heidi and Mazel, Sharon. *What to Expect When You're Expecting*. New York: Workman Publishing Company, Inc., 2008

Myers, David G. and Diener, Ed, *Who is Happy?* American Psychological Society, Vol. 6, No. 1, January 1995

Nettleton, Sarah. *The Simple Home: the luxury of enough*. Connecticut: The Taunton Press, 2007

Pollen, Stephen M. and Levin, Mark. *Die Broke*. New York: HarperBusiness, 1997

Schechter, Harriet. *Let Go of Clutter*. New York: McGraw-Hill, 2001

Schor, Juliet. *Do Americans Shop Too Much?* Massachusetts: Beacon Press, 2000

Smallin, Donna. *Organizing Plain & Simple*. Massachusetts: Storey Publishing, LLC, 2002

Susanka, Sarah. *the not so big life: making room for what really matters*. New York: Random House, 2007

Tolin, David, Frost, Randy and Steketee, Gail. *Buried in Treasures: Help for Acquiring, Saving and Hoarding.* New York: Oxford University Press, Inc., 2007

Waddill, Kathy. *The Organizing Sourcebook: Nine strategies for simplifying your life.* New York, McGraw-Hill, 2001

Walsh, Peter. *Enough Already: Clearing Mental Clutter to Become the Best You.* New York: Free Press, 2009

Walsh, Peter. *It's All Too Much: An Easy Plan for Living a Richer Life with Less Stuff.* New York: Free Press, 2007

Webb, Martha and Zackheim, Sarah. *Dress your House for Success.* New York: Three Rivers Press, 1997

WEBSITE ADDRESSES

www.41pounds.org	organization dedicated to eliminating 80-95% of junk mail
www.agreatergift.org	ethical fair trade gift and crafts products from a range of developing countries
www.altgifts.org	give a gift in honor of someone
www.AnnualCreditReport.com	site set up by the three big credit reporting agencies in the United States to furnish free annual credit reports as required by federal law
www.antshe.org	Association of Nontraditional Students in Higher Education
www.BestBuy.com	trade-in or recycle electronics
www.betterworldbooks.com	get a great deal on books while funding literacy
www.booksforafrica.org	collects, sorts, ships, and distributes books to children in Africa
www.booksforsoldiers.com	ships books, DVDs and supplies to deployed soldiers and soldiers in hospitals via a volunteer network

www.bringmeabook.org	provides easy access to the best children's books and inspires reading aloud to children
www.bullfrogfilms.com	leading US publisher of independently- produced, environmental DVDs and videos
www.CafePress.com	custom t-shirts, personalized gifts, posters and art, mugs, and more to support charities
www.catalogchoice.org	control catalogs and unsolicited snail mail
www.celebrateyourphotos.net	helps people preserve and enjoy their photos
www. CertifiedProfessionalOrganizers. org	BCPO® Certification is a voluntary, industry-led effort that benefits the members of the organizing profession as well as the public
www.clutterersanonymous.net	CLA is a fellowship of men and women who share their experience, strength, and hope with each other to solve their common problem with clutter and help each other to recover

www.clutterless.org	their philosophy complements the work of counselors and organizers and teaches clutterers how to unclutter their emotions
www. commercialfreechildhood.org	CCFC is the only national organization devoted to limiting the impact of commercial culture on children
www.couponcabin.com	free coupon codes, printable coupons, and deals to over 3,300 stores
www.couponmom.com	grocery, printable, and online coupon database
www.coupons.com	grocery, printable, codes, local, Internet, and restaurant coupons
www.Craigslist.com	post free local ads online
www.CreativeMemories.com	career opportunity selling photo-safe scrapbook albums
www.CreditKarma.com	receive your free credit score
www.dmetraining.com	DME Training and Consulting teaches practical and easy-to-learn ideas and techniques to people who are seeking to improve their lives

www.donate.worldvision.org	Christian organization dedicated to working with children, families, and communities to overcome poverty and injustice
www.earth911.org	how to recycle just about anything close to where you live
www.eBay.com	sell your items to a world market
www.e-mealz.com	delicious weekly meal plans
www.equifax.com	one of the three major credit bureaus
www.experian.com	one of the three major credit bureaus
www.FAFSA.com	Free Application for Federal Student Aid
www.FlyLady.net	personal online coaching with the Fly Lady to manage and organize your home
www.folusa.org	Friends of the Library
www.freecycle.com	post free local ads online
www.freedomfiler.com	home filing system
www.give.org	check out the reputation of charities
www.goodwill.org	Goodwill Industries, Inc.

www.greenschools.net	nonprofit organization established to improve the health of schools
www.habitat.org	Habitat for Humanity
www.heifer.org	nonprofit organization whose goal is to help end world hunger and poverty through self-reliance and sustainability
www.heartofamerica.org	nonprofit organization providing all children with the tools to read
www.heritagemakers.com	preserve and showcase photographs
www.hesperian.org	develops and distributes health materials around the world
www.hrblock.com	H&R Block
www.iamfoundation.org	empower children and adults worldwide through publishing and gifting books and music
www.ikea.com	Scandinavian modern style furniture, accessories, and storage options
www.intlbookproject.org	International Book Project
www.irs.gov	Internal Revenue Service
www.irs.ustreas.gov	U.S. Treasury

www.irs.ustreas.gov/prod/forms_pubs	IRS publications and forms
www.Job.com	job search site
www.justgive.org	online charitable giving
www.LinkedIn.com	build your professional network
www.LiveCareer.com	career builder and resume templates
www.mealsmatter.org	nutrition facts and meals to help you live a healthier life
www.messies.com	Messies Anonymous support group
www.Monster.com	job search and resume tips
www.MotherNatureNetwork.com	resource for daily environmental news and green commentary
www.moversguide.usps.com	United States Postal Service
www.moving.org	American Moving and Storage Association
www.napo.net	National Association of Professional Organizers
www.neat.com/products	NeatReceipts scanner
www.newgrowth.com	give a tree as a gift
www.nsgcd.org	National Study Group on Chronic Disorganization

www.obviously.com/junkmail	stop junk mail, e-mail, and phone calls
www.ocfoundation.org	International Obsessive Compulsive Disorder Foundation
www.onlineorganizing.com	tips and blogs written by professional organizers
www.optoutprescreen.com	joint venture among credit bureaus to allow customer to opt out of receiving credit card solicitations
www.oxfamamericaunwrapped.com	nonprofit organization that helps create lasting solutions to poverty, hunger, and injustice
www.paperretriever.com	paper recycling program designed for civic groups, schools, and large employers to raise funds through recycling
www.RachaelRay.com	recipes and kitchen basics
www.ResumeBuilder.com	build the perfect resume
www.SafeCosmetics.org	nonprofit dedicated to eliminating chemicals in cosmetics
www.salvationarmyusa.com	Salvation Army
www.SaveMyPix.com	transfer paper photographs to digital
www.secretsanta.com	free online gift exchange event planner

www.Selfstorage.org	Self Storage Association
www.SendOutCards.com/vali	Internet card software sends real cards; send a trial card for free
www.shoeboxed.com	organize receipts, business cards, and bills online
www.shopathome.com	coupons for 1000's of brand names
www.Shopgreen.pricegrabber.com	natural, organic, and earth-friendly products
www.Shutterfly.com	organize digital photos online
www.Snapfish.com	organize digital photos online
www.Soles4Souls.org	charity for recycling shoes for people in need
www.thecluttercrew.com	Vali's business website
www.theclutterdiet.com	online help with clutter from professional organizers
www.thegreenguide.com	shopping, saving, and greening your lifestyle from National Geographic's Green Guide
www.thepapertiger.com	web-based document management software and filing system product
www.thestoryofstuff.org	The Story of Stuff website

www.transunion.com	one of the three major credit bureaus
www.treasurydirect.gov	order government savings bonds
www.ugandangold.com	<u>supports coffee</u> farms in Uganda
www.wellsfargo.com	list of paper documents to save
www.writeaprisoner.com/ books-behind-bars	posts requests from prison libraries
www.YellowPages.com	Yellow Pages online

WEB REFERENCES

1   Self Storage Association, "Fact Sheet," http://www. selfstorage.org/ssa/Content/NavigationMenu/ AboutSSA/FactSheet/default.htm. 6/30/11

2   Federal Reserve's G.19 report on consumer credit, released July 2011, http://www.creditcards.com/credit-card-news/credit-card-industry-facts-personal-debt-statistics-1276.php. 5/2011

3   American Forest and Paper Association, 2009, http:// www.statmill.org/PressRelArchive.asp

4   American Forest and Paper Association, 2009, http:// www.statmill.org/PressRelArchive.asp

5   Environment Canada, http://www.ec.gc.ca/default. asp?lang=En&n=FD9B0E51-1

6   Wells Fargo Advisors, LLC, "What to keep, where to store and when to shred," 2009, http://www.pwm.wfadv.com/ files/11881/What%20to%20keep,%20where%20to%20 store%20and%20when%20to%20shred.pdf

7   IRS Publication 526, Charitable Contributions, http:// www.irs.gov/pub/irs-pdf/p526.pdf

8   IRS Publication 561: Determining the Value of Donated Property, http://www.irs.gov/pub/irs-pdf/p561.pdf

9   IRS Publication 552: Recordkeeping for Individuals, http://www.irs.gov/pub/irs-pdf/p552.pdf

10   Kaikati, Andrew M. and Kaikati, Jack G., "Let's Make a Deal," January 25, 2010, Wall Street Journal, http://online.wsj.com/article/SB1000142405274870447150457444468 92208327428.html

11   Seeking Alpha, Sound Money Tips, http://seekingalpha.com/article/7277-tip-on-getting-the-best-return-on-home-improvements

12   Baskind, Chris, "5 reasons not to drink bottled water," Mother Nature Network, March 15, 2010, http://www.mnn.com/food/healthy-eating/stories/5-reasons-not-to-drink-bottled-water#

13   Leonard, Annie, "The Story of Stuff," July 12, 2008, http://www.youtube.com/watch?v=gLBE5QAYXp8

14   Dickenson, David K., Bridges to literacy, 1991, http://www.heartofamerica.org/literacy.htm

15   McQuillan, Jeff, the Literacy Crisis, California State University, 1998, http://www.heartofamerica.org/literacy.htm

16   McQuillan, Jeff, the Literacy Crisis, California State University, 1998, http://www.heartofamerica.org/literacy.htm

17   McQuillan, Jeff, the Literacy Crisis, California State University, 1998, http://www.heartofamerica.org/literacy.htm

[18] McQuillan, Jeff, the Literacy Crisis, California State University, 1998, http://www.heartofamerica.org/literacy.htm

[19] IRS Publication 526, Charitable Contributions, http://www.irs.gov/pub/irs-pdf/p526.pdf

[20] IRS Publication 561: Determining the Value of Donated Property, http://www.irs.gov/pub/irs-pdf/p561.pdf

[21] IRS form 8283, Noncash Charitable Contributions, http://www.irs.gov/pub/irs-pdf/f8283.pdf

[22] Salvation Army, Donation Value Guide, http://www.satruck.org/donation-value-guide

[23] Goodwill Industries, Valuation Guide for Goodwill Donors, http://www.goodwill.org/wp-content/uploads/2010/12/Donation_Valuation_Guide.pdf

[24] National Center for Education Statistics, Institute of Education Sciences, http://nces.ed.gov/fastfacts/display.asp?id=51

[25] Leonard, Annie, "The Story of Stuff," July 12, 2008, http://www.youtube.com/watch?v=gLBE5QAYXp8

[26] Mall of America, 2012, http://www.mallofamerica.com/about/moa/facts

[27] SkyscraperPage.com, 2012, http://skyscraperpage.com/cities/?buildingID=28

[28] Stanbor, Zak, "U.S. web sales grow solidly for QVC.com in 2009," Vertical Web Media, March 1, 2010, http://www.

Organize This!

internetretailer.com/2010/03/01/u-s-web-sales-grow-solidly-for-qvc-com-in-2009

29 Smith, Lisa, "The Truth About Real Estate Prices," Investopedia, January 7, 2011, http://www.investopedia.com/articles/mortages-real-estate/11/the-truth-about-the-real-estate-market.asp#axzz1evgs4Dt7

30 Japanese Ministry of Internal Affairs and Communications, Housing and Land Survey, 2003, http://en.wikipedia.org/wiki/Housing_in_Japan

31 Griswold, Kent, "Ikea and Small Space Solutions," Tiny-HouseBlog.com, October 12, 2011, http://tinyhouseblog.com/tiny-house-video/ ikea-and-small-space-solutions/

32 Roden, PhD, Patrick, "Peter Pan House: Homes not built to take into account the needs of elderly residents," AginginPlace.com, January 2009, http://aginginplace.com/2009/01/peter-pan-housing/